Walter Jackson Bate

Negative Capability

The Intuitive Approach in Keats

Introduction by Maura Del Serra

ERIS

ERIS

265 Riverside Drive
New York, NY 10025

First Contra Mundum Press edition 2012
Originally published in 1939 by Harvard University Press.
Reprinted with permission of the Estate of W.J. Bate.

ISBN 978-1-971559-38-4

Contents

Acknowledgments

To Converse Owen Smith to whom its subject is no stranger, this little volume is sincerely inscribed.

A Polar Star That Never Closes its Eyes

Maura Del Serra

Shelley's famous statement proclaiming that poets are "the unacknowledged legislators of the world," is, in Keats's case, not only true but also exceedingly moving: the "Adonais" celebrated in Shelley's epicedium is remembered by history as the young neoclassical-romantic genius, author of the "Ode on a Grecian Urn." For the last two centuries, Keats has occupied a fiery winged seat in the sky of fixed stars, those "bright stars" not only of English poetry (as he aspired to in life) but of the Western literary canon *tout court.* As Hölderlin before and Rilke after—who can be considered one of his heirs—Keats understood and lived poetry as a celebration and an absolute vocation, a lucidly oracular daemon of the primeval sacred, a Muse-Music of the unfathomable reality that ties the ephemeral to the eternal, the infernal dimension to the Elysian one, the merciless clamor of History and Power to the magical and silent eloquence of a Good that, platonically speaking, is considered the prerequisite for composing authentic poetry, and that is transposed into the hendiadys Beauty-Truth by way of the twin and specular dichotomy of Eros and Thanatos (Life and

Death, pleasure and pain, celebrated also by Leopardi). It is a theoretical knot that transplanted the classic tragedy into the Baroque *Streben* and then into European Romanticism. In the Anglo-Saxon world, the same knot was translated into the symbolism and decadent aestheticism of Ruskin and Pater, of the Pre-Raphaelites and Wilde, of Yeats and Wallace Stevens. All these poets had their "own" Keats (while in Italy his message was understood only—although superficially—by the young D'Annunzio, especially in his 1882 *Canto Novo*).

The noble, secluded self-awareness of "Junkets"—as his mentor Hunt jokingly called him—led him to "love human nature" and to "write in Man's honor"—according to the ethical and social enthusiasm of the time, influenced by enlightened philanthropy—, although he did not want "men to touch" what he wrote, to contaminate and distort it with their ideological utilitarianism (from his letter to Haydon dated December 22, 1818).

The life and work of Keats, from his biographical, lyrical, and speculative "adult cradle," which he identified with his Scottish tour in the summer of 1817, to the final Roman cradle-tomb of February 1821, by now marked by the forced refusal of writing and the temptation of suicide, run literally at the speed of his creative light and are characterized by what he called "allegory" or "allegorical life" (that is, symbolical). In his opinion, such a life ideal belonged only to his beloved Shakespeare, his perennial and unsurpassable source of inspiration—unlike Spenser and Milton—because of his metaphorical and lyrical-rhythmic *imagery* (see the letter-diary to his siblings

George and Georgiana dated February 14–May 3, 1819). This allegorical life, of which his works constitute the splendid glosses, implied an ascetic as well as tormented self-liberation from the "egotistical sublime," whose most famous representatives were Byron and, although in a more complex and persuasive manner, the first admired and then criticized Wordsworth. It required a progressive de-personalization, both spiritual and psychological, a sympathetic objectification that was all encompassing and capable of projecting itself onto all other beings and things in nature. Keats's sculpted poetic de-personalization, "hammered" by the tough biographical vicissitudes—orphanhood, the untimely death of his brother Tom, the crude critical reviews of his "Endymion," his tormented love for Fanny Brawne—is carried out in the name of "Poetry's naturalness" and in that of the poet himself, different from the "dreamer." Such an idea will be famously, but more ambiguously paralleled by Rimbaud's *voyant* of the "Je est un autre"; by Mallarmé's wish for a "disparition élocutoire du poète"; by Pessoa's trans-personal and multiple identity characterized by heteronomies and "abdication"; by Heidegger's *Gelassenheit*, which he in turn inherited from Hölderlin and Rilke by way of the "pure nothing" of Meister Eckhart; and we should not forget Katherine Mansfield's extreme determination to become, in her stories, "more duck than the duck, more apple than the apple," as well as Eliot's creative ethos. The latter admired Keats's "acumen and the depth of observation he scattered throughout his letters," and remarked how "there is hardly one statement of Keats about poetry, which

[...] will not be found to be true." We could add that this holds true for every great poet, even though the mainstream and popular poetry—which Keats detested—would remain well within the egotistical-sublime tradition, based on demiurgism and supermanism, derived from Cartesian and Leibnizian subjectivism as well as the *Sturm und Drang* and German idealism.

Keats's empathic universalization is sensuously plastic in its covering the flesh of reality not with foresight but with visionary sight, which constitutes the objective correlative—to use Eliot's formula—of the poet's famous "Negative Capability," investigated in the now classic yet still unparalleled study by Walter Jackson Bate, which has been republished here. In it, the author reveals his meticulous zeal, remaining *tout entier à sa proie attaché* with a sort of linear devotion. This rather concrete theory, which Keats had been developing and which was finalized in his maturation between 1817–18, was best expressed not in his lyrical poems—as we all know, he detested didactic poetry, which has "a palpable design upon us," and which does not "enter the soul" (from the letter to Reynolds, dated February 3, 1818)—but rather in his splendid and vibrant letters, and in one particular letter to Woodhouse dated October 27, 1818. There, Keats states that the "chameleon poet" is an entity without a Self, "it is not itself—it has no self—it is everything and nothing. [...] A Poet is the most unpoetical of anything in existence; because he has no identity—he is continually in for—and filling some other Body—The Sun, the Moon, the Sea and Men and Women who are creatures of impulse are poetical and have about them an unchangeable attribute—the poet has none; no identity..."

This "flight from personality," as Eliot defined it exploring its ethical and aesthetic consequences, recalls also Musil's Anders (Other, Different), later normalized into Ulrich, the protagonist of his *Mann ohne Eigenschaften* (the man without qualities, without personal characteristics), or the anonymous-autobiographical "K" in Kafka's *Trial*. However, the philosophical and theological origins of this idea are based—more or less intuitively, given Keats's vast autodidactic training—on Heraclitus' purified "dry soul," on Pythagorean doctrine—among whom Philolaus defined friendship (according to what Keats called an elective relation) as "the common thought of separate thinkers"—but also on Origen's complete and "heretical" free-will and Pico della Mirandola's concept of chameleonic man "animal of a varied nature, multiform and shifting being"; or even, according to the most benevolent and mind boggling theories of the Jewish Kabbalah, on the *tzimtzum*, that is God's retreat from the world he created so it can truly exist "on its own."

The poet is de-personalized through the empathic "affections of the heart" and the creative imagination capable of translating beauty (which is identified with the Fancy-gardener), the giver of order that is truthful in and of itself like "Adam's dream" (from the letter to Bailey dated November 22, 1817). This beauty can be identified with the "noble insects," with the spider creator of lightness, with the sparrow that pecks the pebbles and rests on the window-sill. It can also, following Blake, lead to "the burden of Mystery"—that is, the natural Sacred—harbinger of the highest level of micro and macro understanding, dissipating, with its elusive awareness, the constantly looming solipsistic cerebral "fog," as Keats states in his short lyrical manifesto "Where's the Poet? Show Him! show Him!" Keats's Muse, in her analogical richness, is anti-erudite and anti-intellectual ("Unintellectual, yet divine to me" from the song "To Fanny"), and strongly campaigns against Pope's "rocking horse" disguised as an Acadian Pegasus ("Sleep and Poetry"), as well as against the materialistic and bourgeois pragmatism of his proto-industrial age.

His Negative Capability, on the contrary, is based on a contemplative, solitary "indolence," devoid of misanthropy, which closely resembles the Taoist *wu-wei* (non-action) that lends a mythical dimension to the evocative Memory. To Indolence, he dedicated an ode ("Ode on Indolence"), which he wrote, along with almost all the others, in that *annus mirabilis* 1818, and which is par-alleled by "What Can I Do to Drive Away" (with its "Petrarchan" rejection of real love in favor of its dream image) as well as by the "Ode on Melancholy." In these two twin odes, Keats—an ex-surgeon—appropriates the Elizabethan legacy of Burton's *Anatomy of Melancholy* through the refined analysis of transient human treasures (Joy that takes her leave with a hand over her mouth, Beauty "that must die"). Through Indolence, the poet evokes the three disquieting allegorical figures that appeared to him in profile, rotating as if in a relief on a "marble urn," sister to the more famous "Grecian Urn." These hooded, praying figures, which would later be-come cherished by the Pre-Raphaelites—Love, Ambition, and the beloved "my demon Poesy"—bear a striking resemblance to Dante's song *Tre donne intorno al cor mi son venute* [Three Women Have Come Round my Heart] from his *Rime*; but are also reminiscent of the rows of souls and the decorated reliefs found in *Purgatorio*: they are visualized by the poet in the fateful hour, and are finally exorcised as if they were *angheloi* of a false ataraxic tranquility and of a pre-Baudelairian dimension predicated on a hypnotic *plazer*, capable of chasing away the "annoy" of noisy and paralyzing mediocrity: "O, for an age so shelter'd from annoy, / That I may never know how change the moons, / Or hear the voice of busy common-sense!" Undoubtedly, this "annoy"—which Keats uses in the sense of a strong discomfort modeled after the Provençal "*enueg*," the opposite of *plazar*—is a pre- cursor to Baudelaire's *spleen* (and he will turn it into the banner of the urban *dandy*). However, this "boredom" appeared also in Leopardi's *Zibaldone*, where it was called the "pure desire for happiness."

At the same time, in the self-therapeutic twin "Ode on Melancholy," Keats struggles to evoke the catharsis from the famous saturnine and depressive condition (the "wakeful anguish" and the "sorrow's mysteries") not by immersing himself in a nullifying Lethe, but rather, as in the "Ode to a Nightingale," by transforming himself into the impersonal and immortal beauty of Nature's cycles (the simple flowers, the wave's rainbow) and into the "beautiful" energies dissipated by a negative passion, the "rich anger" of the beloved woman. In the letter to his brothers

George and Thomas dated September 21, 1817, Keats states confidently that in "a great poet the sense of Beauty overcomes every other consideration, or rather obliterates all consideration," and defines the Shakespearean Negative Capability as the ability to inhabit "uncertainties, mysteries, doubts, without any irritable reaching after fact and reason." It is an ability more specifically defined as indolence and a receptive passivity in the following letter to Reynolds dated February 9, 1818, where the frenzy of the Mercury-bee is skillfully juxtaposed against the stillness of the Jupiter-flower: "Now it is more noble to sit like Jove than to fly like Mercury:—let us not therefore go hurrying about and collecting honey, bee-like, buzzing here and there impatiently from a knowledge of what is to be arrived at. But let us open our leaves like a flower, and be passive and receptive; budding patiently under the eye of Apollo and taking hints from every noble insect that favours us with a visit—Sap will be given us for meat, and dew for drink" (this recalls the same stillness of "non-action" that Emily Dickinson evoked in "The Grass so Little Has to Do"). His radical anti-clericalism—based on the ides of Hazlitt, Godwin, and Shelley and expressed in the poem *Written in Disgust of Vulgar Superstition*—will evolve rapidly in an *epochè* rigorous and at the same time anti-ideological, more stoic than post-illuminist. In much the same way, the immature romantic love for an "easeful Death," considered an escape from reality—which characterizes Keats's Spencerian and "Gothic" period ("The Eve of St. Mark," "The Eve of St. Agnes," "La Belle dame sans merci," "Isabella")—will grow, in 1818, into a more mature and articulated "system for the education of the soul [...] more valid than the Christian one." That is, an understanding of the world not as a sorrowful "Vale of Tears," but rather as an evolutionary "Vale of Soul-Making" (from the letter-journal entry dated February 14–May 3 1819, addressed to his siblings George and Georgiana), dedicated to converting the impersonal Intelligence into a Soul or individual consciousness (and this soul-Making will be remembered, in the 20th century, by Jung and Hillman). The letter concludes with a strongly assertive rhetorical question: "I will call the *world* a School instituted for the purpose of teaching little children to read—I will call the *human heart* the *horn Book* used in that school—and I will call *the Child able to read, the Soul* made from that *school* and its *hornbook*. Do you not see how necessary a World of Pains and Troubles is to school an Intelligence and make it a soul? [...] Not merely is the Heart a Hornbook, It is the Mind's Bible, it is the Minds experience, it is the teat from which the mind or intelligence sucks its identity—".

Keats's fulminating ethical and aesthetic evolution, with his plans of studying in solitude and "writing freely but judiciously" and with discipline (from the letter to Sarah Jeffrey dated June 19, 1819), derive from a vision of himself as a self-deprecating "philosopher" and humanistic "priest" of the Soul ("Ode to Psyche"), and from a vision of fame as fierce miscreed and of Fantasy as "deceiving elf" ("Ode to a Nightingale"). These ideas led to a poetic tryptic that includes the aforementioned "Where's the Poet? Show Him! Show Him!"—characterized by a universalistic and at the same time pre-Nietzschean atmosphere (" 'Tis the man who with a man / Is an equal, be he king, / Or poorest of the beggar-clan, / Or any other wondrous thing / A man may be 'twixt ape and Plato; / 'Tis the man who with a bird, / Wren or eagle, finds his way to / All its instincts; [...]")—"Welcome Joy, and welcome Sorrow"—which recalls Goethe and owes a great debt to the Book of Job, "Lethe's weed, and Hermes' feather, / [...] I do love you both together! / [...] Fair and foul I love together; / Meadows sweet where flames burn under;" and here Keats borrows from *Macbeth*'s song of witches, with their famous chaotic reversal ("Fair is foul, and foul is fair"), which is however treated in a pre-Freudian synthesis of Apollonian & Dionysian, conscious and unconscious—and finally "Why did I laugh tonight? No voice will tell"—which is the mirror of the love suffering caused by Fanny (as shown by the extreme lyrics and supplicant letters)—marked by the sweetness of pain and bearing the seal of death like "life's high meed," which, in its telos, even surpasses the cherished "verse, fame, and beauty."

The poet's dismissal of his own life, made "posthumous" by sickness and disenchantment, is sealed by the ascetic maxim, "My Imagination is a Monastery and I am its Monk" (from the letter to Shelley dated 1820, in which Keats tries to convince him to be less abstract and "more artist"). And the letter to Fanny dated 1820 sounds like the "double" of his famous self-epitaph dictated to Severn, and appears to be a less desperate but perhaps more moving final testament: "'If I should die,' said I to myself, 'I have left no immortal work behind me—nothing to make my friends proud of my memory—but I have loved the principle of Beauty in all things, and if I had had time I would have made myself remember'd.'"

In turn, the lyrical mirror of this disenchanted and resolute dismissal is the extreme "Ode to Autumn," in which the Negative Capability leads to an almost complete disappearance of the Self from a generous, sweet, and fruitful nature, which is dominated by the soothing and chaste "stubble plains" in place of the unripe "songs of spring." The same images run through the letter to Reynolds dated September 21, 1819: "chaste weather, Dian skies. I never lik'd the stubble fields so much as now—" And they will appear again, in the negative, in the "dry grass singing" of Eliot's *Waste Land* ("What the Thunder Said").

Keats's other great legacy—which he paid for in a literal way and upfront with his life—is that of having evoked, with an extraordinarily lucid greatness, the laws and the deep reality of the human condition, in order to combat the illusions, the lies, the hypocrisies, and the vanity that—as Simone Weil would show—poison and blind the soul: this is a point of view that shares the same substance as the cosmic and natural sacred, resembling a polar star that never closes its eyes, which constitutes the color of its light and the sound of its voice, a river that flows toward its estuary and at the same time toward its source, toward the continuous origin that beats in the rhythm of the human pulse, covering the mortals with the flesh of myth and the blood of knowledge.

Maura Del Serra

The excellence of every art is its intensity, capable of making all disagreeables evaporate from their being in close relationship with Beauty and Truth. [...] Several things dove-tailed in my mind, and at once it struck me what quality went to form a Man of Achievement, especially in Literature, and which Shakespeare possessed so enormously—I mean *Negative Capability*, that is, when a man is capable of being in uncertainties, mysteries, doubts, without any irritable reaching after fact and reason—Coleridge, for instance, would let go by a fine isolated verisimilitude caught from the Penetralium of mystery, from being incapable of remaining content with half-knowledge. This pursued through volumes would perhaps take us no further than this, that with a great poet the sense of Beauty overcomes every other consideration, or rather obliterates all consideration.

KEATS, Letter to George & Thomas Keats, December 21, 1817

To know a thing, what we can call knowing, a man must first *love* the thing, sympathise with it.

CARLYLE, *The Hero as Poet*

Keats certainly had more of the penetrative and sympathetic imagination which belongs to the poet, of that imagination which identifies itself with the momentary object of its contemplation, than any man of these later days.

JAMES RUSSELL LOWELL, *Keats*

Ebenso ist es mit einem Dichter. Solange er bloß seine wenigen subjectiven Empfindungen ausspricht, ist er noch keiner zu nennen; aber sobald er die Welt sich anzueignen und auszusprechen weiß, ist er ein Poet.

ECKERMANN, *Gespräche mit Goethe*

Negative Capability

The Intuitive Approach in Keats

Introductory Note

The letters of Keats have elicited considerable study and analysis, particularly during the last two or three decades. The attention has been well bestowed. For few poets have been gifted with a more penetrating insight into the workings of their art than that which Keats possessed; and, with the exception of a few marginal annotations, the entire body of Keats's criticism is to be found only in his letters.

Concentrated analysis of the letters, however, may still prove rewarding. For Keats's discussions of poetry revolve to a large degree about his conception of the nature of the artist's character and his approach to his subject; and room certainly remains for further examination of Keats's conception of the poetical character accompanied by illustration from his own work. The quality which characterizes both the poet and his approach Keats designated by the term, *Negative Capability*; and it is the critical articulation of the philosophy of *Negative Capability*, Keats's own abidance by it, and the peculiar bent of mind which gave rise to it, which I have essayed to clarify and describe.

I wish to express my indebtedness for many helpful suggestions to Professors John Livingston Lowes, John Nash Douglas Bush, and Robert Hillyer, to Mr. Philip A. Smith, and to my tutor, Mr. Charles A. Steel.

Publisher's Note

In general, the 1939 Harvard University Press edition of Bate's original text has been replicated as is; however, several minor alterations have been made to the text:

Instead of retaining italics in poem titles, as Bate had them, such have been put in quotes;

Brackets have been added around ellipses and footnotes have been made into endnotes;

In addition, and most significantly, wherever Bate regularized Keats's punctuation (eliminating dashes, adding periods, question marks, etc.) and made it uniform, erasing its idiosyncratic character, it has been restored;

Finally, English translations from Bergson's *Creative Evolution* have been added in brackets, following the original French, which Bate quoted in his premier publication.

I

The Truth of the Imagination

The exclamation, "O for a Life of Sensations rather than of Thoughts," has too often been quoted out of context. It occurs in an early letter to Benjamin Bailey, in what is perhaps Keats's first extant discussion of the Imagination:

> I am certain of nothing but the holiness of the Heart's affections and the truth of the Imagination—What the Imagination seizes as Beauty must be truth—whether it existed before or not,—[...] The Imagination may be compared to Adam's dream,—he awoke and found it truth:—I am more zealous in this affair, because I have never yet been able to perceive how anything can be known for truth by consequitive [sic] reasoning—and yet it must be—Can it be that even the greatest Philosopher ever arrived at his Goal without putting aside numerous objections—However it may be, O for a Life of Sensations rather than of Thoughts![1]

This passage contains Keats's first distinction between the logical element of the intellect and the imaginative, intuitive faculty, and his insistence not merely that the use of the Imagination is the more efficacious means of arriving at truth but that it is actually the only way by which truth can be grasped. "Consequitive reasoning" is the power of categorizing and representing objects as externally related to one another. It is almost *quantitative*, so to speak, embracing what is measurable; it is mediate, in contrast to the Imagination, which is intuitive and immediate; it analyzes rather than synthesizes, and it dissects rather than creates. It is essentially an outward view of phenomena, and never succeeds in grasping the reality within. The Imagination is the direct opposite: it looks inward, grasping by an effort of sympathy and intuition the hidden intention and reality of life; and what it seizes, synthesizes, and creates "must be truth—whether it existed before or not."

This arbitrary division of the Imagination and the logical faculty, with an insistence on the greater validity of the former, has been paralleled during the present generation by Bergson's thesis that the intellect and the instinct are turned in opposite directions—the former towards inert matter and the latter towards life.[2] There is, as it were, a definite *geometrical tendency* in the intellect:

> L'intelligence, telle que Kant nous la représente, baigne dans une atmosphère de spatialité à laquelle elle est aussi inséparablement unie que le corps vivant à l'air qu'il respire. Nos perceptions ne nous arrivent qu'après avoir traversé cette atmosphère. Elles s'y sont imprégnées par avance de notre géométrie, de sorte que notre faculté de penser ne fait que retrouver, dans la matière, les propriétiés mathématiques qu'y a déposées par avance notre faculté de percevoir.[3]
>
> [Intelligence, as Kant represents it to us, is bathed in an atmosphere of spatiality to which it is as inseparably united as the living body to the air it breathes. Our perceptions reach us only after having passed

through this atmosphere. They have been impregnated in advance by our geometry, so that our faculty of thinking only finds again in matter the mathematical properties which our faculty of perceiving has already deposed there.]

The Intellect, which is essentially categorical, remains outside of phenomena, taking from this external position the greatest number of views which it possibly can. It draws life into its own rigid molds, giving it an artificial order, and brings it to us only after translating it into terms of inertia. Instinct, on the other hand, enters life, grasping the intention and simple movement which connect it and give it significance:

L'intelligence, par l'intermédiaire de la science qui est son oeuvre, nous livrera de plus en plus complètement le secret des opérations physiques; de la vie elle ne nous apporte, et ne prétend d'ailleurs nous apporter, qu'une traduction en termes d'inertie. Elle tourne tout autour, prenant, du dehors, le plus grand nombre possible de vues sur cet objet qu'elle attire chez elle, au lieu d'entrer chez lui. Mais c'est à l'intérieur même de la vie que nous conduirait l'intuition, je veux dire l'instinct devenu désintéressé, conscient de lui-même, capable de réfléchir sur son objet et de l'élargir indéfiniment.[1]

[Intelligence, by means of science, which is its work, will deliver up to us more and more completely the secret of physical operations; of life it brings us and moreover only claims to bring us a translation in terms of inertia. It goes all round life, taking from outside the greatest possible number of views of it, drawing it into itself instead of entering into it. But it is to the very inwardness of life that intuition leads us, by intuition I mean instinct that has become disinterested, self-conscious, capable of reflect-ing upon its object and of enlarging it indefinitely.]

The logical element of the intellect can no more know life than it can conceive of the progress of movement. It concerns itself with *immobility*; and immobility is only *apparent*. In its contemplation of movement, for example, the intellect can direct itself only to past, present, and future positions; it represents becoming as a static series; and when it tries to form an idea of movement, it does so only by reconstructing from a sequence of immobilities.[5] Instinct, however, by what might be called a "divining sympathy" can grasp the hidden significance and force at work beneath phenomena:

> Quelle que soit la force que se traduit dans la genèse du système nerveux de la Chenille, nous ne l'atteignons, avec nos yeux et notre intelligence, que comme une juxtaposition de nerfs et de centres nerveux. [...] [But it can be known] par une intuition (vécue plutot que représentée) qui ressemble sans doute à ce qui s'appelle chez nous sympathie divinatrice.[6]

> [Whatever be the force that is at work in the genesis of the nervous system of the caterpillar, to our eyes and our intelligence it is only a juxtaposition of nerves and nervous centres. [...] [But it can be known]

by an intuition (lived rather than represented), which is probably like what we call divining sympathy.]

The regaining, by an effort of sympathetic intuition, of the intention that runs beneath life, is the task of the artist: "C'est cette intention que l'artiste vise à ressaisir en se repliçant à l'intérieur de l'objet par une espèce de sympathie, en abaissant, par un effort d'intuition, la barrière que l'espace interpose entre lui et le modèle."[7] ["This intention is just what the artist tries to regain by a kind of sympathy, in breaking down, by an effort of intuition, the barrier that space puts up between him and his model."]

I have ventured to recapitulate Bergson's distinction between intuition and the intellect for the purpose of clarifying Keats's theory of the poetical character, which anticipates, to a striking degree, Bergson's own thesis. "Consequitive reasoning" is for Keats an essentially artificial process; it is at home only in the mathematical, measurable world of its own construction. "What the Imagination," on the other hand, "seizes as Beauty must be Truth." The Imagination enters life,[8] identifying itself momentarily with the object of its contemplation; and it has only—as Hazlitt said of Shakespeare—"to think of anything in order to become that thing, with all the circumstances belonging to it."[9] "Consequitive reasoning," however, draws life out into itself, into its own already constructed molds, distorting it to fit the shapes of these molds. It deduces, analyzes, compresses, and reshapes.

A "consequitive man,"[10] who searches for a truth by means of "consequitive reasoning," shuts himself up in a circle of articulated formulae, premises and results, definitions and conclusions. The poet who possesses the quality of *Negative Capability* will be "capable of being in uncertainties, mysteries, doubts, *without any irritable reaching after fact and reason*";[11] and it is precisely this "irritable reaching after fact and reason" which characterizes the search of the "consequitive man" for truth, until it is small wonder that

> ...the dull brain perplexes and retards.

Coleridge, says Keats in the same passage, exemplifies the "consequitive man" who pursues truth in this fashion: "Coleridge, for instance, would let go by a fine isolated verisimilitude caught from the Penetralium of mystery, from being incapable of remaining content with half-knowledge." Poetic truth, precisely because it is glimpsed only intuitively, can never be seen and known with a clarity and accuracy sufficient to satisfy the exacting demand of the logical faculty; there is always about it an air of "uncertainties, mysteries, doubts," of "half-knowledge." And Coleridge, after having momentarily broken through the barrier which space puts between the artist and his object, and glimpsed "a fine isolated verisimilitude caught from the Penetralium of mystery,"—Coleridge, says Keats, seeks to justify this "verisimilitude" intellectually, with an "irritable reaching after fact and reason," and to dissociate from it the air of "uncertainties," "mysteries," and "half-knowledge"; he demands that each of the rigid molds of his logical faculty be satisfactorily filled by the truth or phenomena which he is contemplating; and because he is unsuccessful in his attempt, he allows the poetic "verisimilitude" which he has grasped to dissipate itself.

The inability of the "consequitive man" to remain "content with half-knowledge" is owing, in large part, to his determination to "make up his mind about everything." In a letter to his brother George, Keats instances his friend, Dilke, as a "consequitive man":

> He thinks of nothing but his "Political Justice"[12] and his Boy. Now the first political duty a Man ought to have a Mind to is the happiness of his friends. I wrote Brown a comment on the subject,[13] wherein I explained what I thought of Dilke's character. Which resolved itself into this conclusion. That Dilke was a man who cannot feel he has a personal identity unless he has made up his Mind about everything. The only means of strengthening one's intellect is to make up one's mind about nothing—to let the mind be a thoroughfare for all thoughts. Not a select party. The genius is not scarce in population. All the stubborn arguers you meet with are of the same brood. They never begin upon a subject they have not preresolved on. [...] Dilke will never come at a truth as long as he lives; because he is always trying at it.[14]

Keats, in this discussion of Dilke, is again suggesting that the "consequitive man," in contemplating phenomena through a logical screen, imposes an artificial order and arrangement upon what he sees.

Keats intimated that Wordsworth's poetry had a "palpable design"[15] upon the reader; and it may be said that the reason, in its attempted approach to truth, has a "palpable design" upon the phenomena which it contemplates.

"Consequitive reasoning," moreover, will not arrive at truth because it is consciously deliberate in its attempt: "Dilke will never come at a truth as long as he lives; because he is always trying at it." The reason sets out on its search for truth with something of a "palpable design" upon the object of its contemplation, regarding it with a hawk's eye, with the intentness of a praying-mantis; and it rejects as unsatisfactory any "fine isolated verisimilitude caught from the Penetralium of mystery" precisely because of the aura of "half-knowledge" surrounding that verisimilitude. The approach of the analytical, rational element of the intellect is voluntary and deliberate—that is to say, conscious. Consciousness is proportionate with the power of choice; it lights up the zone of possibilities and potential activity which surround and encompass an act or thought;[16] and hesitation, deliberation, and choice are its accompaniments.

In contradistinction to the approach of the intellect, that of the Imagination is unconscious and without deliberation and choice; and the riveting of itself to that which it embraces is immediate—its function, that is to say, is *instinctive*.[17] In a letter to his brother George, Keats wrote:

> The greater part of Men make their way with the same instinctiveness, the same unwandering eye

> from their purposes, the same animal eagerness as the Hawk—[...] I go among the Fields and catch a glimpse of a Stoat or a fieldmouse peeping out of the withered grass—the creature hath a purpose and its eyes are bright with it. But then, as Wordsworth says, "we have all one human heart"—there is an ellectric [sic] fire in human nature tending to purify—so that among these human creatures there is continually some birth of a new heroism—The pity is that we must wonder at it: as we should at finding a pearl in rubbish—[...] Even here[18] though I myself am pursuing the same instinctive course as the veriest human animal you can think of—I am, however, young writing at random—straining at particles of light in the midst of a great darkness—without knowing the bearing of any one assertion, of any one opinion—yet may I not in this be free from sin? May there not be superior beings amused with any graceful though instinctive attitude my mind may fall into, as I am entertained with the alertness of a Stoat or the anxiety of a Deer?[19]

The Imagination is almost animal-like in its instinctive approach to truth; it "has a purpose and its eyes are bright with it." There is an echo here of the earlier characterization of *Negative Capability* as the quality which distinguishes the poet who approaches his object immediately and intuitively, glimpsing a "fine isolated verisimilitude caught from the Penetralium of mystery," and remaining content with the "half-knowledge" with which he has been favored. Keats here is attempting to follow precisely the same line of procedure: "I myself am pursuing the same instinctive course as the veriest human animal you can think of [...] straining at particles of light in the midst of a great darkness—without knowing the bearing of any one assertion, of any one opinion—"

This intuitive, imaginative element of the mind is essentially synthetic, not only in the concrete shaping and expression of truth but in its momentary seizure of truth as well. It is synthetic in its grasping of truth because it does not, like the reason, detect only particular attributes and qualities; it penetrates beyond the external, and by a momentary divining sympathy, "feels upon its pulse,"[20] as it were, the hidden movement and intention which lie beneath. The Imagination "struggles," says Coleridge, "to idealize and unify. It is essentially *vital*, even as all objects (*as* objects) are essentially fixed and dead."[21] Through a kind of fellow-feeling rather than from articulate and logical representation, it comprehends, grasps, and *feels* the peculiar force at work within the object of its contemplation. It conceives rather than perceives; its function will be that, almost, of a *common sense*, in the Aristotelian sense of a faculty in which the various reports of the several senses are reduced to a common apperception; and it will grasp an object with all the qualities and attributes of that object amalgamating and fusing themselves into a concrete unity of a general sensation or conception.

It is precisely because of this embracing, conceiving quality which characterizes its apprehension of truth that what the Imagination seizes "must be truth—whether it existed before or not"; for into the Imagination's apprehension of its object are woven the very subtlest threads of association, which escape the scrutiny of the intellect but which strike, however faintly, a common emotional note, which the logic may not detect but which the intuition will feel. These concomitant associations blend into chords of feeling which are not analyzed, picked apart, or dissociated from the phenomenon which they surround. They will be united and intermingled with the fusion already gained by the Imagination, the function of which is in character so essentially like that of a *common sense*; for they will form an insepa-rable part of the truth of that phenomenon, and are a necessary accompaniment of a true poetic insight;[22] and the Imagination, in this sense, will look upon "the Sun the Moon the Stars, the Earth and its contents, as materials to form greater things—that is to say ethereal things."[23]

This imaginative, highly intuitive faculty is to be trusted above all else. "Consequitive reasoning," in its abstraction, is an artificial construction; and real-ity cannot be "settled" to fit its rigid scaffolding:

Oh, never will the prize
High reason, and the love of good and ill,
Be my award! Things cannot to the will
Be settled, but they tease us out of thought;[24]

"Reason," as Coleridge wrote, "is aloof from time and space; the Imagination has control over both."[25] Mobility and immobility alike are its subjects; and the fusion of the two, the union of quality and quan-tity, the Imagination alone can feel and conceive; for it seizes and explains creation in terms of creation, and life, in terms of life.

It is for this reason that a "life of Sensations"—or, as Keats might have said, of "intuitions"—is to be preferred to a life "of thoughts."

II

The Sympathetic Nature of the Poetical Character

The approach of the Imagination to truth is intuitive and immediate because of its penetration of the barrier which space puts between it and the object of its contemplation; and the penetration of this barrier, or the breaking down of it, is achieved through the momentary identification of the Imagination with its object—that is, through *sympathy*.

The poet may manifest such sympathy, and subsequently obtain the poetic insight which is its reward, only if he himself is passive in character. Keats wrote to Reynolds that "Poetry should be *great & unobtrusive*, a thing which enters into one's soul, and does not startle and amaze with itself, but with its subject";[26] and we may say that the poet himself is "unobtrusive" in character, and, by negating his own identity, capable of "entering into the soul" of his "subject." It will be remembered from Keats's criticism of Dilke that the mark of the "consequitive man" is that he "cannot feel he has a personal identity until he has made up his Mind about everything."[27] The poet, however, "the Man of Achievement—especially in Literature," whose distinguishing attribute is the quality of *Negative Capability*,[28] will have no such insistent desire to "feel his own identity"; he will "make up his mind about nothing"; he will "let his mind be a thoroughfare for all thoughts"; there will be no "irritable reaching after fact and reason"; and he will remember that,

It is a flaw
In happiness, to see beyond our bourn—
It forces us in summer skies to mourn,
It spoils the singing of the Nightingale.[29]

In one of his earliest extant letters, the same in which he exclaimed, "O for a Life of Sensations rather than of Thoughts," Keats wrote to Bailey, "Men of Genius are great as certain ethereal Chemicals operat- ing on the Mass of neutral intellect—by [*for* but] they have not any individuality, any determined character."[30] For the poet in particular, a "lack of determined charac-ter" is a necessity. Wordsworth, for all his "wise passiveness," offends on this score because of his "systematic unwillingness"—to use Hazlitt's phrase about him—"to share the palm with his subject."[31] The character of Wordsworth, says Keats, stands in direct contrast to that of Shakespeare, and may be called the "egotistical sublime";[32] and the accompaniments of its assertive individuality are "egotism, vanity, and bigotry."[33] In a manner reminiscent of many passages in Hazlitt's review of the *Excursion*,[34] Keats, in a letter to Reynolds, condemns Wordsworth's obtrusive subjectivity:

> for the sake of a few fine or domestic passages, are we to be bullied into a certain Philosophy engendered in the whims of an Egotist—Every man has his speculations, but every man does not brood[35] and peacock over them till he makes a false coinage and deceives himself—[...] We hate poetry that has a palpable design upon us—and if we do not agree, seems to put its hand in its breeches pocket. Poetry should be great

> & unobtrusive, a thing which enters into one's soul, and does not startle or amaze with itself but with its subject.—How beautiful are the retired flowers! how would they lose their beauty were they to throng into the highway, crying out, "admire me I am a violet!—dote upon me I am a primrose!" [...] Old Matthew spoke to him a few years ago on some nothing, & because he happens in an Evening Walk to imagine the figure of an Old Man—he must stamp it down in black and white, and it is henceforth sacred—[36]

This "Wordsworthian or egotistical sublime" subjectivity "is a thing *per se* and stands alone."[37] Its approach is deliberate, conscious, and with something of a "palpable design." When possessed by a great personality, such a quality is good in itself; but the willfulness of its selection, which results from the consciousness of its procedure, will necessarily be incomplete and unrepresentative. It will be partial precisely because it does select; for selection implies choice, and choice is dependent upon the whim of the poet's subjective personality:

> Now it is more noble to sit like Jove than to fly like Mercury—let us not therefore go hurrying about and collecting honey, bee-like, buzzing here and there impatiently from a knowledge of what is to be arrived at; but let us open our leaves like a flower and be passive and receptive—budding patiently under the eye of Apollo and taking hints from every noble insect that favors us with a visit—[38]

The poet who obtrudes his own identity raises an additional barrier between himself and his subject: he will be in no position, certainly, to be "with Achilles shouting in the Trenches, or with Theocritus in the Vales of Sicily";[39] or, if a sparrow comes before his window, to "take part in its existence and pick about the Gravel";[40] and, after having so identified himself with his subject, "not dispute or assert but whisper results to his neighbor."[41] Such a manifestation of the poetic gift will be permitted only to the poet who possesses the quality of *Negative Capability*, who is himself characterless and without identity, who will not only tolerate but unhesitatingly welcome the obliteration of himself by the life about him, and, with the truth thus gained, rest content. This is the philosophy, not of Wordsworth or Milton, but of Shakespeare, and of Keats himself.

We know that Keats attended Hazlitt's "Lectures on the English Poets," given early in 1818,[42] and he wrote to Bailey on January 23 that he definitely intended to hear the third of this series of lectures, which was to be given on the twenty-seventh of the month.[43] The subject of Hazlitt's lecture was "Shakespeare and Milton"; and a considerable portion of the discussion of Shakespeare was devoted to an insistence upon the essentially negative quality of Shakespeare's own character:

> He was the least of an egotist that it was possible to be. He was nothing in himself; but he was all that others were, or that they could become. He not only had in himself the germs of every faculty and feeling, but he could follow them by anticipation, intuitively,

> into all their conceivable ramifications, through every change of fortune, or conflict of passion, or turn of thought. [...] He had only to think of anything in order to become that thing, with all the circumstances belonging to it.[44]

Keats listened with care whenever Hazlitt spoke, and he remembered what Hazlitt said about the characterless nature of Shakespeare. It was an expansion and a more definite articulation of what he himself had felt a month before when he wrote to his brothers that *Negative Capability* was a quality "which Shakespeare possessed so enormously."[45] The influence of this lecture of Hazlitt's makes itself manifest in a letter to Woodhouse, written in October of the same year. This letter is perhaps the most definite statement we have from Keats on his own view of the poetical character:

> As to the poetical Character itself (I mean that sort of which, if I am anything, I am a Member; that sort distinguished from the Wordsworthian or egotistical sublime; which is a thing per se and stands alone) it is not itself—it has no self—it is everything and nothing—It has no character—it enjoys light and shade; it lives in gusto, be it foul or fair, high or low, rich or poor, mean or elevated—It has as much delight in conceiving an Iago as an Imogen. What shocks the virtuous Philosopher, delights the camelion [sic] Poet. It does no harm from its relish of the dark side of things any more than from its taste for the bright one; because they both end in speculation. A Poet is the most unpoetical of anything in existence; because

> he has no Identity—he is continually in, for—and filling some other Body—The Sun, the Moon, the Sea and Men and Women who are creatures of impulse are poetical and have about them an unchangeable attribute—the poet has none; no identity—he is certainly the most unpoetical of all God's creatures. [...] When I am in a room with People if ever I am free from speculating on creations of my own brain, then not myself goes home to myself; but the identity of everyone in the room begins to press upon me that I am in a very little time an[ni]hilated—not only among Men, it would be the same in a Nursery of children.[46]

It is this being forever "in, for, & filling some other body" that is the reward of the characterless poet; for the truth thus acquired can never be gained otherwise. The negative poetical character will grasp the nature of an Iago because it *is* Iago, and it will conceive the truth of an Imogen because it has become Imogen; and tolerance, acceptance, and forgiveness will accompany this understanding, as they could never have done had the mind approached either of them categorically and rationally with a determination already resolved upon, and with its own identity obtrusively projecting itself. And this self-annihilation of the poet through a sympathetic identification of himself with his subject—whether a creature or a phenomenon—will be accomplished through the Imagination, immediately and intuitively.[47]

This capacity of the poet for what might be called *Einfüllung* is dwelt upon also in a little-known lyric entitled "The Poet: A Fragment," which is found among both the Woodhouse and the George Keats transcripts, and which was written at about the same time as the passage just quoted from the letter to Woodhouse:

Where's the Poet? show him! show him,
Muses nine! that I may know him!
'Tis the man who with a man
Is an equal, be he king
Or poorest of the beggar-clan,
Or any other wondrous thing
A man may be 'twixt ape and Plato;
'Tis the man who with a bird,
Wren or Eagle, finds his way to
All its instincts; he hath heard
The lion's roaring, and can tell
What his horny throat expresseth,
And to him the Tiger's yell
Comes articulate and presseth
On his ear like mother-tongue.

Here again is an insistence upon the impartiality and indiscriminate acceptance of the poet. More than that, however, we find a clearer statement of the reason why an instinctive sympathy is better able to grasp truth than is "consequitive reasoning." The poet is,

...the man who with a bird,
Wren or Eagle, finds his way to
All its instincts;

And it is precisely this that logical and scientific analysis, *per se*, cannot do.

But experience and knowledge are necessary for the poet, whatever the object of his contemplation. "Fancy" alone is of little value to the poet; it is a "deceiving elf,"[48] divorced from life; and when it gains ascendancy, poetry becomes little more than "a mere Jack a lanthen [sic] to amuse whoever may chance to be struck with its brilliance."[49] "A long poem," wrote Keats to Bailey, "is a test of Invention which I take to be the Polar Star of Poetry, as Fancy is the Sails, and Imagination the Rudder."[50] "Fancy" is certain to shipwreck the poet unless he has as his rudder, as his guide, the Imagination—a unifying, conceiving, and intuitive faculty which has a firm grip upon actuality, and into which a deep and rich store both of knowledge and experience has entered and become a part; and it must support the Imagination, of which it is indeed a part, and not supplant it:

> An extensive knowledge is needful to thinking people—[...] The difference of high Sensations with and without knowledge appears to me this—in the latter case we are falling continually ten thousand fathoms deep and being blown up again, without wings, and with all the horror of a bare shouldered creature—in the former case, our shoulders are fledge, and we go thro' the same air and space without fear.[51]

About a week before writing this passage, Keats wrote to his publisher, Taylor:

> I know nothing I have read nothing and I mean to follow Solomon's directions of "get Wisdom—get understanding"—I find cavalier days are gone by. [...]—there is but one way for me—the road lies th[r] ough application study and thought.[52]

Three days later, Keats had written to Reynolds:

> I have written to George for some Books—shall learn Greek, and very likely Italian—and in other ways prepare myself to ask Hazlitt in about a year's time the best metaphysical road I can take.[53]

But personal experience, he wrote in the same letter, is also necessary: "there is something else wanting to one who passes his life among Books." And in his next letter to Reynolds, written a week later, he further insists upon the necessity of experience for sympathetic understanding:

> for axioms in philosophy are not axioms until they are proved upon our pulses: We read fine———things but never feel them to the full until we have gone the same steps as the Author.— [...] Until we are sick, we understand not;—in fine, as Byron says, "Knowledge is Sorrow"; and I go on to say that "Sorrow is Wisdom"—[54]

"Nothing ever becomes real," he wrote to his brother George, "till it is experienced—Even a Proverb is no proverb to you till your Life has illustrated it."[55] He criticizes "Isabella" because of the "inexperience of life" shown in it;[56] and, in speaking of his projected walking-tour of Scotland, he wrote to Bailey,

> I should not have consented to myself these four months tramping in the highlands but that I thought it would give me more experience, rub off more Prejudice, use [me] to more hardship, identify finer scenes load me with grander Mountains, and strengthen more my reach in Poetry, than would stopping at home among Books even though I should read Homer—[57]

Pain and sorrow are inextricably woven into the texture of life. For the poet to know life, it is necessary that he understand suffering as well as joy; and for him to understand suffering, it is necessary that he himself experience it—"Until we are sick, we understand not."[58] The poet may not linger in the "realm" "of Flora and old Pan";[59] for after having enumerated the pleasures of that place, Keats writes:

> And can I ever bid these joys farewell?
> Yes, I must pass them for a nobler life,
> Where I may find the agonies, the strife
> Of human hearts.[60]

For life may be compared to a mansion of many rooms; and the poet's progress through this mansion necessitates his passage through the "Chamber of Maiden-Thought," where he himself first suffers and comes to understand the pain which is bound up with life.[61] The sorrow which is first felt and understood in this "Chamber of Maiden-Thought" is an essential part of the making of the poet. For without it, he would "fly like Mercury [...] bee-like buzzing here and there impatiently," and not "sit like Jove [...] passive and receptive,"[62] contemplating with an understanding eye, and feeling with a sympathetic heart; he would be only a spark of "intelligence," as it were, and not a "Soul":

> Call the world if you Please "The vale of Soul-making" [...] I say "Soul making" soul as distinguished from an Intelligence—There may be intelligences or sparks of the divinity in millions—but they are not Souls till they acquire identities, till each one is personally itself. Intelligences are atoms of perception—they know and they see and they are pure, in short they are God—how then are Souls to be made? How then are these sparks which are God to have identity given them—[...] How, but by the medium of a world like this?[63]

The experience and knowledge thus gained in this "vale of Soul-making" will form an essential part of the intuitive and sympathetic approach of the poet; and in this sense, too, a "Life of Sensations" is to be preferred to a life "of Thoughts." For the experience gained in the world is of a highly practical nature, and is a truer means of acquiring knowledge than may be gained through isolation;[64] and Keats's use of the word "Sensation" throughout his letters is almost always with its traditional empirical meaning,[65] and may possibly have been borrowed from Hartley either directly or through conversation with Hazlitt, Hunt, or Woodhouse.[66]

The knowledge and experience thus gained in the world will deepen and enlarge the heart, and will intensify the heart's capacity to sympathize, understand, and express:

> I will call the world [Keats writes in the same letter] a School instituted for the purpose of teaching little children to read—I will call the human heart the horn Book used in that School—and I will call the Child able to read, the Soul made from that School and its hornbook. Do you not see how necessary a World of Pains and troubles is to school an Intelligence and make it a Soul? A Place where the heart must feel and suffer in a thousand diverse ways! Not merely is the Heart a Hornbook, It is the Mind's Bible, it is the Mind's experience, it is the text from which the Mind or Intelligence sucks its identity.[67]

This excerpt occurs in Keats's long journal letter to his brother (February 14 to May 3, 1819). On the day that he began this letter, Keats wrote, "I have not gone on with 'Hyperion'."[68] The highly idealistic humanism of "Hyperion"—especially of the first two books—had little meaning for him any longer. It was on the sixteenth of April that he wrote the passage just quoted. Four days later he gave up "Hyperion," and handed the unfinished manuscript to Woodhouse.

Even as early as "Endymion,"[69] there is an insistence that truth may never be acquired through self-centered isolation. Endymion's lonely search after the ideal is restless, painful, and fruitless. He rids himself of his selfish seclusion, and is relieved from his restlessness, only after he has been moved to sympathy for the ill-fated lovers, Alpheus and Arethusa, and prays[70] that their sufferings may be assuaged.

But it is the revised "Hyperion"—the "Fall of Hyperion, A Dream"—written in September, 1819, that contains Keats's most definite insistence upon the necessity of suffering. According to the interpretation of Robert Bridges, the temple in which the poet awakes is the "temple of Knowledge."[71] The temple may at least be said to represent Truth, and the poet may not enter it until he has ceased to be a "visionary," recovered from his state of selfish isolation, and acquired an active sympathy with the pain and miseries of the world. For

> "None can usurp this height," returned that shade,
> "But those to whom the miseries of the world
> Are misery, and will not let them rest."[72]

The steps to the altar are the struggle of the poet to acquire that height. This struggle will consist of repeated pain and suffering until the poet feels "What 'tis to die and live again."[73] For the world is a "vale of Soul-making"—"A Place where the heart must feel and suffer in a thousand diverse ways";[74] and it is by this "dying into life," this annihilation of himself through an active sympathy with his fellow creatures, that the poet achieves his own soul.[75] Middleton Murry has maintained that, by the time of the writing of the revised "Hyperion," the quality of *Negative Capability* has come to have a somewhat broader application:

> For this supreme quality there is no familiar name; few people save Keats have even suspected its existence. For the moral quality we can find a word; it is

> more than tolerance, it is forgiveness. It is that quality which Christ preeminently possessed. But for this other kind of forgiveness, a forgiveness which forgives not only men but life itself, not only the pains which men inflict, but the pains which are knit up in the very nature of existence, we have no word. We have, as yet, scarcely even a sense of the quality itself. Let it be called, though the word cannot fail to be misunderstood, Acceptance.[76]

There is an element of truth in this criticism. But we must guard against reading into Keats an idealism which is not there. What distinguishes Keats from his contemporaries, and from almost all the other major English poets except Shakespeare, is the highly empirical nature of his philosophy. It is necessary that the quality of *Negative Capability* confine itself, at least in its manifestation, to the particular; if it extends overmuch to the ideal realm, the poet will tend to become an abstract reasoner and obtrude his own views,[77] he will become *reflective* rather than *creative*, to use Ruskin's distinction,[78] and he will lose the strong grasp upon actualities, the firm sense of the solid world, which is the most noteworthy manifestation of the objective and characterless poet. The prophetess, Moneta, in the revised "Hyperion," bids the poet, if he would not be a "dreamer,"[79] extend his sympathy to the particular and the concrete, and not to think overmuch—as Middleton Murry would have him do—of "the pains which are knit up in the very nature of existence"; for the true benefactors of humanity

"are no vision'ries,"
Rejoin'd that voice—"They are no dreamers weak,
They seek no wonder but the human face,
No music but a happy-noted voice—"[80]

"Thou art a dreaming thing,
A fever of thyself—think of the Earth."[81]

The experience thus gained in the world will enlarge the mind and the heart of the poet; and it is necessary that it be had if the poet is to be no mere "dreamer," "falling continually ten thousand fathoms deep and being blown up again without wings,"[82] or being propel-led along by the "Fancy" without the very necessary "rudder" of the Imagination.[83] Each individual experience and each particle of knowledge, no matter how fine and subtle to avail separately in logical analysis and judgment, will become a part of the imaginative, intuitive faculty which grasps, synthesizes, and expresses truth; and they will form a very necessary and essential part of the intuitive and sympathetic approach of the poet.

The whole of this experience and knowledge will come to focus upon the object which the poet contemplates and with which he attempts to identify himself. The selection of materials which the Imagination seizes upon in the concrete shaping of its insight will be made by an intuitive faculty which has synthesized this knowledge, and which approaches its selection in a manner not dissimilar to the intuitive judgment of William James's "expert"[84] or Newman's "illative sense"[85]—by an intuition, that is to say, which, deepened and enriched by a store of experience which has become a part of it, acts as an instinctive, unerring touchstone.

For the true poet will not only conceive of an Iago or an Imogen, of "the Sun, the Moon, the Sea and Men and Women," as Keats said in the letter to Woodhouse, with a cordial hand, as it were, extended to each. It is not enough for the artist to view his model—whether a creature or an object—with a generous and warm feeling about the heart. His conception must involve a very active participation in the existence, work, and fortune of the object towards which he has extended his sympathy. If a sparrow comes before his window, it is not enough that the poet regard the sparrow with something of a tolerant, half-amused liberality; feeling pleasantly and generously disposed to the sparrow is not active-sympathy. He must not only become the sparrow, but he must *work* with it; and there must be an *Einfühlung*, as it were, as well as an *Einfüllung*, so that he can "take part in its existence and pick about the Gravel."[86] By such an imaginative and sympathetic *Einfühlung*, the poet will grasp the truth of the creature as the analytical mind may not—that is, he

> "finds his way to
> All its instincts;"

The feeling experienced by the sparrow as it spreads its wings will be revealed to him. Those actions, if any, which are deliberate on the part of the sparrow, and those which are impulsive, will be understood by him; for he, too, will perform them. And those sensations experienced by the sparrow as it swallows a seed of grain, or as it treads upon the gravel, with the claws of each of its feet clutching a pebble as it stoops to pick, will, by a fellow-living, be experienced by the poet, too; and the poet, as a consequence, will comprehend a truth which escapes the exacting scrutiny of "consequitive reasoning."

A sympathy such as this, for all its intuitiveness, is an *intelligent* sympathy. The threads of all past experience are unconsciously woven into the intuition which directs it; and the greater and more vital such experience, the sounder and more understanding is the sympathy. The more knowledge the poet has about the sparrow, its bodily construction and its ways of life, the more complete will be his capacity to "find his way" into the sparrow, providing that this knowledge does not become detached from the living creature before him, and assume an artificial and abstract existence in itself. "The Sun, the Moon, the Sea and Men and Women"—these things are *poetical* and have identities of their own. And the *truth* of each of these "identities," a conception of the varying fortune, progress, and actual *living* of each creature and each phenomenon through every turn of circumstance that attends upon the flow of the passing second—these will press upon the sympathetic and receptive mind—and heart—of the poet until his own individuality becomes "in a very little time annihilated," and he is at last at one with them; and the poet, who will rest "content with half-knowledge" and will manifest no "irritable reaching after fact and reason," whose heart has been deepened by suffering, and who has been schooled by knowledge and experience, will discover with a flash of intuition the peculiar nature and truth of these "identities," and will speak out this truth in imperishable phrase. For the poet *is* the object, endowed with a means of expressing itself.

III

Intensity and the Concrete

There is a strain in Keats, said A. C. Bradley, which "may be called the Shakespearean strain, and it works against any inclination to erect walls between the ideal and real."[87] The statement is well made; for if Keats is idealistic, his idealism is concrete. A view of the world as a "vale of Soul-making," as a "School" in which "the heart must feel and suffer in a thousand diverse ways," is an idealization, perhaps; for it is symbolizing a natural process as an embodiment of a higher excellence. But it must be noted that Keats never separates and abstracts this excellence from the process itself. What to him was an embodiment of the ideal must be accepted and cherished as the only means of knowing the ideal.

For the philosophy of *Negative Capability* looks upon the concrete as the manifestation, the working out, of the ideal. Keats wrote of Milton, in his copy of *Paradise Lost*, "There was working in him as it were that same sort of thing as operates in the great world to the end of a Prophecy's being accomplished";[88] and it is in the "great world" that the ideal accomplishes itself, and makes itself known. Pain and conflict have a meaning; they are the working out of an ideal, and that which they produce is a similar working out. Their excellence consists in the soul which they fashion; and that of the soul, thus fashioned, in its ability to sympathize, understand, and aid.[89] It is precisely on this point that the idealism of Keats is so different from that of Shelley. Shelley regarded pain and conflict with horror; they were indications for him of how far man yet was from attaining the ideal. For Keats, however, the pain and suffering felt in the "vale of Soul-making," "the agonies, the strife of human hearts,"[90] had a meaning; and for the poet to regard them as obstacles to the ideal would be to obtrude his own identity, his own views, and not, certainly, to "let his mind be a thoroughfare for all thoughts." And these manifestations of the ideal—"The Sun, the Moon, the Sea and Men and Women"—these, for Keats, are the concern of the poet; these he must accept, resting content with his "half-knowledge"; these he must conceive, with all their qualities and attributes fusing into a concrete totality; by an intuitive working of the Imagination, he must grasp the life, the force, which is at work within them; and, through an annihilation of his own identity, become a part of them, and speak out the truth of each. It is in this sense that "an artist must serve Mammon."[91]

For the concrete—and here we strike at once to the very core of Keats's conception of poetry and of life—the concrete and the ideal are one and the same. If the particular is lost in the universal, the life and force which the artist seeks to recapture will melt in his grasp; and it is precisely this life, this hidden intensity and force, which the poet must feel and portray if he is to find truth and express it. "The excellence of every Art," wrote Keats, "is its intensity, capable of making all disagreeables evaporate, from their being in close relationship with Beauty & Truth—"[92] This intensity is the concentrated life, force, and meaning of a particular. Keats wrote to

Shelley, "you might curb your magnanimity, and be more of an artist, and load every rift of your subject with ore."[93] It is by a concentration, not an expansion, of force and intensity that the poet simultaneously rejoices the Imagination and the intellect with a beauty, a truth; and the poet must take care never to divorce this intensity from the particular, or it will lose the strength it so surely acquires from its imprisonment within the concrete.

A love of the concrete, and a trust in the energy, the truth, confined within it, were deeply imbedded in Keats's mind. The most cursory perusal of his manuscript revisions illustrates his intuitive working towards concrete concentration. The opening of the eighth stanza of the "Eve of St. Agnes," for example, was originally written

> She danc'd along with vague uneager look,
> Her anxious lips mouth full pulp'd with rosy thoughts.

Keats at once crossed out "look" and substituted "eyes," and by degrees transformed the weak prettiness of the second line into something approaching "intensity": "Anxious her lips, her breathing quick and short." The phrase, "the wing of evening tiger-moths," in the casement stanza, he concentrated into the "tiger-moth's deep-damask'd wings." "Unclasps her *bosom* jewels" he intensified into "Unclasps her *warmèd* jewels." In the feast stanza, Keats originally wrote

> While he from forth the closet brought a heap
> Of candied sweets...

Keats at once perceived the lack of strength in "sweets," and he crossed it out and put the more specific "fruits" above it. But "fruits," even, was not sufficiently concrete; and so he enumerated individually

> ... candied apple, quince, and plum, and gourd;
> With jellies soother than the dairy curd.

"Dairy curd" became the more concrete "creamy curd," and "lucent syrops smooth with cinnamon" was strengthened by the substitution of "tinct" for "smooth."[94]

Intensity, for Keats, was almost physical in its nature; and for that reason, too, intensity, to his mind, should be kept within the bounds of the concrete. Keats's delight in concentrated physical intensity is well exemplified by the frequency of his use of such words as "ache" and "pant."[95] It is illustrated, too, in his underlinings in Shakespeare. A few lines, all characterized by a physical intensity of feeling, and all heavily marked and underlined by Keats, may be instanced from *The Tempest* alone:[96]

> O, the cry did knock
> Against my very heart![97]

> For still 'tis beating in my mind, [...][98]

> Do not infest your mind with beating on
> The strangeness of this business.[99]

A turn or two I'll walk
To still my beating mind.[100]

There is a tendency in Keats, moreover, in his instinctive working towards intensity, to ally his sensory images more closely with the sense of touch, and thus makes them stronger and more concrete. Arthur Symons, in speaking of Keats's strong grasp upon the solid world, said that he had a "firm common sense of the imagination."[101] In my attempt to clarify Keats's conception of the function of the Imagination, I have used the term *common sense* with a somewhat broader application—in its Aristotelian meaning of a faculty in which the reports of the various senses are united and fused into a common apperception, a faculty which conceives rather than perceives, and brings to bear upon one point all the resources of the several senses. It is only in Keats's maturest work that instances of this Aristotelian common sense may be found; and these are rare. But there is throughout the whole of his work a tendency towards what might be called a confusion of the senses, which is much the same thing but of a less definite, less refined, nature; for even as early as "Sleep and Poetry," Keats expressed his desire in rendering expression of a phenomenon to

Write on my tablets all that was permitted,
All that was for our human senses fitted.[102]

Keats uses the words "fragrant" or "fragrance," for example, not only in reference to odors, but to visual images as well:

Through bowers of fragrant and enwreathèd light.[103]

He gives it an almost tactile quality:

In fragrance soft and coolness to the eye,[104]

Or he uses it, again, in such varied ways as:

The inward fragrance of each other's hearts.[105]

'Mid hush'd, cool-rooted flowers, fragrant-eyed.[106]

Other instances of this "confusion of the senses," which has so strongly influenced subsequent poetry, often for the worst, are: "smoothest silence,"[107] "pale and silver silence,"[108] "embalmèd darkness,"[109] "shadows of melodious utterance,"[110] "incense-pillowed,"[111] "purple riot,"[112] and "scarlet pain."[113]

This "confusion of the senses," this common-sense working of the Imagination, is an accompaniment, perhaps a part, of Keats's strong tendency towards tactile imagery, his craving a touch, for the concrete.[114] "Touch," he wrote, "has a memory";[115] and much of his imagery is an attempt to solidify the impressions of his senses by giving them a tactile strength. Thus he makes incense almost tangible by calling it "soft" and picturing it as *hanging*:

I cannot see what flowers are at my feet
Nor what soft incense hangs upon the boughs,[116]

Or again, to take three similar instances from the "Fall of Hyperion":

Soft-showering in my ears), and, (by the touch
Of scent,)[117]

As the *moist scent* of flowers,[118]

Shifts sudden to the south, the small warm rain
Melts out the frozen incense from all flowers,[119]

Nor does Keats confine this common-sense fusion of the senses to epithets or to single phrases. He sometimes condenses within one or two lines several images, each addressed to a different sense. Thus, in one line, we have an appeal to the senses of sight, touch, and hearing:

Pale, latticed, chill, and silent as a tomb.[120]

Or to the senses of sight, smell, and touch:

And like a rose in vermeil tint and shape,
In fragrance soft and coolness to the eye,[121]

Or to four distinct senses in

'Mid hush'd, cool-rooted flowers, fragrant-eyed,[122]

and in

In the retired quiet of the night,
Filling the chilly room with perfume light.[123]

Accompanying this common-sense fusion of images, and developing out of the same tendency for intense condensation, is Keats's ability to endow his epithets with startling sympathetic touches. Bridges has remarked upon this:

> In one respect he is in my opinion superior to Milton, for his descriptive touches are more sympathetic and less conventional. To give an example, where he describes Asia, he has
>
> "More thought than woe was in her dusky face,
> For she was prophesying of her glory;"
>
> In my first edition I said that Milton would not have put in this epithet dusky. It happens that in Paradise Regained (IV, 76) [...] he uses this very word of the Indians:
>
> "Dusk faces with white silken Turbans wreathed,"
>
> and this, while it corrects my faulty analysis, well exhibits the difference which I wished to explain. In Milton dusk is the primary external distinction used as a sufficient description; in Keats dusky is secondary, and added on to the emotional expression of the face, and from that it takes a sympathetic warmth which is wholly absent in Milton.[124]

Sympathetic touches of this nature abound in the maturer work of Keats:

> Old ocean rolls a lengthened wave to shore,
> Down whose green back the short-lived foam, all
> hoar,
> Bursts gradual, with a wayward indolence.[125]

And she forgot the stars, the moon, the sun,
  And she forgot the blue above the trees,

She had no knowledge when the day was done,[126]

And scarce three steps, ere Music's golden tongue
Flatter'd to tears this agèd man and poor;[127]
Feebly she laugheth in the languid moon,[128]

Unclasps her warmèd jewels one by one.[129]

His old right hand lay nerveless, listless, dead,
Unsceptred; and his realmless eyes were closed;[130]

Tall oaks, branch-charmèd by the earnest stars,[131]

Savour of poisonous brass and metal sick:[132]

And still they were the same bright, patient stars.[133]

How cams't thou over the unfooted sea?[134]

Now we may lift our bruisèd vizors up,
And take the flattering freshness of the air,[135]

She stood in tears amid the alien corn;[136]

It was a concentration within a particular of the intensity, the beauty, the meaning, the force which is at work within that particular, which gives it identity, and is indeed its nature and its "truth"—it was this hidden and elusive movement, intention, and identity towards which Keats's natural bent in poetry instinctively led him, and which in time became a conscious goal; and from this instinctive reaching out of Keats for intensity come both his gift for bestowing on his epithets an astonishing sympathetic and penetrative revelation of truth and his ability to strengthen his sensory images by allying them more closely with the sense of touch.

This intensity at work beneath the surface was the expression for Keats of the real self, the identity, the truth of a phenomenon. Severn, who accompanied Keats on many of his walks, was often astonished at the acuteness of Keats's observation, but more so, even, at that to which his attention was riveted:

> Nothing seemed to escape him, the song of the bird, the undernote of response from covert to hedge, the rustle of some animal, the changing of the green and brown lights and furtive shadows, the motions of the wind—just how it took certain tall flowers and plants—and the wayfaring of the clouds: even the features and gestures of passing tramps, the colour of one woman's hair, the smile on one child's face, the furtive animalism below the deceptive humanity in many of the vagrants, even the hats, clothes, shoes, wherever these conveyed the remotest hint as to the real self of the wearer.[137]

Now it was precisely this "furtive animalism" of the passing vagrants, "the rustle of some animal," "the motions of the wind—*just how it took certain tall flowers,*"—it was this force at work within, glimpsed momentarily, for example, in the "alertness of a Stoat or the anxiety of a Deer," which for Keats was expression of identity, of individuality, of truth, and in which poetry consisted:

> May there not be superior beings amused with any graceful though instinctive attitude my mind may fall into, as I am entertained with the alertness of a Stoat or the anxiety of a Deer? Though a quarrel in the Streets is a thing to be hated, the energies displayed in it are fine: the commonest Man shows a grace in his quarrel—By a superior being our reasonings may take the same tone—though erroneous they may be fine—This is the very thing in which consists poetry; and if so it is not so fine a thing as philosophy—[138]

This intensity, this peculiar force at work within the object, this almost dynamic expression of identity and truth, is intuitively and almost physically felt by the sympathetic, characterless poet; for the poet *is* the object, and the force at work within the object is also at work within him. It was the physical intensity of the phrase "sea-shouldering whales"[139] which caused it to give Keats such delight on his first reading of the *Faerie Queene*: "He *hoisted* himself up," according to Clarke, "and looked burly and dominant, as he said, 'What an image that is—*sea-shouldering whales*!'"[140] And Keats, entering into the image, doubtless felt press upon his own shoulders the weight of the parting billows.

An admirable instance of this physical intensity in Keats's own work is his description, in the first "Hyperion," of the goddess Thea:

Had stood a pigmy's height: she would have ta'en
Achilles by the hair, and bent his neck;
Or with a finger stay'd Ixion's wheel.[141]

There is an extreme physical intensity concentrated within the first line and a half. There is a picture, almost physically felt, of the look of agony on the face of Achilles, the veins and the muscles standing out from his throat, as the goddess Thea slowly pulls back his head. The third line is undoubtedly one of those lines of "Hyperion" which, said Keats, depend upon the "false beauty proceeding from art" and not on the "true voice of feeling."[142] The line is intended, of course, to show strength; and so it does—of a kind. But the strength is magical, supernatural: Thea calmly lays her finger on Ixion's wheel and it stops. The straining, muscular strength of the first picture is gone.

It has been pointed out that, in contrast to Shelley's epithets, which connote incessant movement and have little in them of fixed outline, those of Keats are essentially *statical*; that they determine rather than suggest, and characterize objects in repose rather than in motion.[143] I should say, however, that the secret of Keats's imagery, the excellence which sets him above his contemporaries in mastery of phrase, is a highly dynamic power momentarily caught at rest and concentrated and imprisoned within an otherwise static image; and that this concentration in Keats is effected with no loss, but indeed with a startling gain, in strength, life, and intensity.

This concentration of energy within a static picture is well illustrated by Keats's frequent use of epithets ending in *ed*. Thus in the line, "Tall oaks, branch-charmèd by the earnest stars,"[144] the branches of the oaks, through the use of the compound, "branch-charmèd," are made the recipient of the energy: the steadily working spell cast by the "earnest stars" becomes concentrated within them until they are heavily charged with intensity. Keats, again, does not write "icy gusts"; he solidifies the gusts, he makes them heavy, by calling them "icèd."[145] Similarly, he does not say "globe shap'd" or "globe-like peonies." He goes farther, and calls the peonies "globèd";[146] and the hand is almost cupping the peony, condensing it further to fit its "globèd" roundness. And in the line and a half,

> So the two brothers and their murdered man
> Rode past fair Florence,[147]

the bold "anticipation of the assassination," as Lamb wrote in his review of the 1820 volume, is wonderfully conceived in one epithet."[148] Or again: in the expression "warmèd jewels,"[149] the jewels are not in the process of being warmed, neither is warmth made a secondary quality through the use of the mere adjective, "warm"; but warmth, rather, has been concentrated within them. And, similarly, in such phrases as "smooth-sculptured stone,"[150] "cool-rooted flowers,"[151] "enwreathèd light,"[152] "over-strainèd might,"[153] "far-foamèd sands,"[154] and—as distinct from "twitch*ing*" and "quiver*ing*"—"palsy-twitched"[155] and "proud-quivered loins"[156] there is a similar concentrated intensity made momentarily static and concrete.

For if Keats paints rather than suggests, and if his images are static rather than moving, that which he paints is intense with concentrated force. "Keats," wrote Ruskin near the end of *Modern Painters*, "(as is his way) puts nearly all that may be said of the pine into one verse, though they are only figurative pines of which he is speaking…

"Far, far around shall those dark-cluster'd trees
  Fledge the wild-ridgèd mountains steep by steep;[157, 158]

In a similar way, all that may be said of homesickness and inarticulate loneliness is concentrated in

Perhaps the self-same song that found a path
  Through the sad heart of Ruth, when, sick for home,
    She stood in tears amid the alien corn;[159]

And again, the lines

And still these two were postured motionless,
Like natural sculpture in cathedral cavern;[160]

are charged with a strength not yet displayed; "But where the dead leaf fell, there did it rest"[161] is heavy with quietness; and the lines,

Until at length old Saturn lifted up
His faded eyes, and saw his kingdom gone,[162]

are weighted with weariness and loss.

"Poesy," wrote Keats in "Sleep and Poetry," is

> the supreme of power
> 'Tis might half slumb'ring on its own right arm.[163]

It is this highly dramatic power, caught momentarily in repose, and restrained and imprisoned still further in the bonds of art, that underlies the satisfying, quiet—but highly intense—completeness of the "Ode on Melancholy" and the ode "To Autumn." And it is precisely this power which characterizes the restrained intensity of the "Ode on a Grecian Urn." For like Cleopatra's

> Eternity was in our lips and eyes,[164]

a line which was marked and underscored by Keats,[165] and which is heavy with the concentration within concrete particulars of all the suggestion eternity can convey, the "Grecian Urn" is weighted with a condensed energy heightened the more because of its compactness; and it, too, is tremulously heavy with an eternity intensified and compressed within a particular.

This intuitive reaching towards a static, yet highly dynamic, conception and expression of the particular is a manifestation, once again, of Keats's instinctive reaching for intensity; and it is an accompaniment, furthermore, of his delight in the concrete and in concentrated physical intensity, his strong tendency towards tactile imagery, the common-sense working of his imagination, and, also, his gift for bestowing on his epithets a sympathetic understanding that both delights and astonishes with its penetrative revelation of truth. And though the acuteness and soundness of Keats's critical insight were chronologically in advance of the excellence of his execution, and he did not live to perform that of which he gave such remarkable promise; and although, too, Keats's own accomplishment in verse is by no means that of a poet who possesses perfectly the quality of *Negative Capability*, yet these manifestations of his reaching for an intensity imprisoned within the bounds of the concrete are indicative of the character of mind that gave rise to his critical philosophy; and a cursory account of the indications of that character of mind has been necessary for a narrowing down of the conception of *Negative Capability* to its actual meaning. For *Negative Capability* is not objectivity nor yet Wordsworth's "wise passiveness," although it is indeed objective and passive in nature. Neither is it an implicit trust in the Imagination nor, even, the Shakespearean quality of annihilating one's own identity by becoming at one with the subject, although these too it includes within its scope. These qualities are rather accompaniments and outgrowths of something more primary which underlies them—an acceptance, as I have been saying, of the particular, a love of it and a trust in it; and an acceptance, moreover, with all its "half-knowledge," of the "sense of Beauty," of force, of intensity, that lies within that particular and is indeed its identity and its truth, and which "overcomes every other consideration, or rather obliterates all consideration."[166] It was this devotion to the intensity imbedded within the concrete which is responsible, not only for the astonishing and penetrative revelations of truth, but also for the heavy richness, the slow, clogged—almost drugged—movement, the choked-in fullness of Keats's finest lines, which gives him a strength with all his luxury, and which keeps his sensuousness firm and vital. And it was this devotion, too, which led him, as he increased in years, to love life with all the gusto of a Chaucer or a Shakespeare, to delight in human beings, whether they were Iagos or Imogens, and to sympathize with them individually and as particulars; for at work within each of them is a nervous and instinctive force, a peculiar identity, which was for Keats their beauty and their truth.

For the "poetical character...lives in gusto, be it foul or fair";[167] and the most heightened zest of all for Keats—and here he is indeed "of Shakespeare's tribe"[168]—was to be found in the living human being: "Scenery is fine," he wrote to Bailey, "but human nature is finer. The Sward is richer for the tread of a real, nervous, english [sic] foot."[169] And it was this *nervous*, this zestful, tremulous reality that became for Keats the greatest of wonders, and beside which the purely fanciful came in time to pale into unreality or drop into insipidity. "Wonders," he wrote to Taylor, shortly after he had made his revision of "Hyperion"—"are no wonders to me. I am more at Home amongst Men and women. I would rather read Chaucer than Ariosto—"[170]

Landor, with unerring instinct, wrote, "What a poet would poor Keats have been, if he had lived! He had something of Shakespeare in him, and (what nobody else ever had) much, very much of Chaucer."[171] The statement is well made; for Keats is of Chaucer's company in his enthusiasm for the life, the gusto, of the particular. A delight in his fellow beings was in Keats's blood. His distinction between the Scotsman and the Irish- man, written during the Scotch tour, is remarkably penetrating in its insight, as is his characterization of Rice, Reynolds, and Richards,[172] or his description, in the same letter, of three imaginary people:

> I know three people of no wit at all, each distinct in his excellence—A, B, and C. A is the soolishest [sic], B the sulkiest, C is a negative—A makes you yawn, B makes you hate, as for C you never see him though he is six feet high.— I bear the first, I forbear the second, I am not certain that the third is. The first is gruel, the second Ditch-water, the third is spilt—he ought to be wiped up. A is inspired by Jack-o'-the-Clock—B has been drilled by a russian [sic] Serjeant, C—they say is not his mother's true Child but that she bought him of a Man who cries, "Young lambs to sell!"[173]

Bradley quotes a portion of this passage and writes:

> C, who is spilt and ought to be wiped up, how often we have met and still shall meet him. Shakespeare, I think, would gladly have fathered the phrase that describes him, and the words that follow are not so much out of the tune of Falstaff.[174]

Keats was vitally aware of the life about him; it pressed upon him, and he both felt it and felt with it. Let us remember the letter to Woodhouse, in which the characterless nature of the poet is so strongly insisted upon:

> When I am in a room with People if ever I am free from speculating on creations of my own brain, then not myself goes home to myself: but the identity of every one in the room begins to press upon me [so] that I am in a very little time an[ni]hilated—not only among Men; it would be the same in a Nursery of children [...][175]

A few weeks before, Keats had written to Dilke, "I wish I could say Tom was any better. *His identity presses upon me* all day so that I am obliged to go out."[176] He could feel the identity of a sparrow, and "pick about the Gravel" with it; and he could feel, too, the trembling withdraw-ing of a snail into its shell:

> He [Shakespeare] has left nothing to say about nothing or any thing: for look at Snails, you know what he says about Snails, you know where he talks about "cockled snails"[177]—well [...] this is in the Venus and Adonis: the Simile brought it to my Mind.
>
> As the snail, whose tender horns being hit,
> Shrinks back into his shelly cave with pain,[178]

Keats could even divine by a fellow-feeling the force at work within a billiard-ball, if we may accredit Woodhouse:

> He has affirmed that he can conceive of a billiard Ball that it may have a sense of delight from its own

> roundness, smoothness & volubility & the rapidity of its motion.[179]

It was precisely this same sensitivity which made him, on reading the phrase "sea-shouldering whales," feel about his own shoulders the weight of the parting billows, and which made him, too, in trying to explain his conception of intensity to Haydon, describe it as "somewhat like the feel I have of Anthony and Cleopatra. Or of Alcibiades, leaning on his Crimson Couch, *his broad shoulders imperceptibly heaving with the Sea.*"[180]

This zest for the real, for the living, is at one with Keats's essential empirical-mindedness; and from this empiricism—for if Keats is idealistic, his idealism is interwoven with the world about him—from this highly empirical nature of Keats comes an ability, likewise Chaucerian, to see things as they are, to regard life with the sane eye of common sense, and to laugh when there is subject for laughter. It will be remembered that Pandarus, in whom Chaucer concentrated so much of his own identity, saw clearly the irony of life and "softe lough." Even during the ten days' wait for Criseyde's return, when he manifests the utmost loyalty and friendship, Pandarus, who is no idealist, can laugh—at Troilus, at the world, and at himself. He is deeply concerned with Troilus's fate, "But in his herte he thoughte and softe lough."[181] "A Man in love," wrote Keats to his brother George, "I do think cuts the sorryest figure in the world—Even when I know a poor fool to be really in pain about it, I could burst out laughing in his Face—"[182] "What a piece of work is man!" said

Hamlet: "How noble in reason! how infinite in faculty! [...] And yet, to me, what is this quintessence of dust?"

There is a wisdom which manifests itself in the ability to look on man as Gulliver did the Lilliputians, noting with a keen and sane eye the ridiculousness of the society and the customs which he has built up, his means of obtaining success, his smugness, his smallness—regarding him indeed as a "poor forked creature,"[183] and yet at the same time feeling a genuine and active sympathy for him and delighting in the life, the instinctive force within him; and this is the wisdom of Chaucer, of Shakespeare, and, had he lived another twenty-five years, it might well have become that of Keats.

For Keats knew well that a "fallible being"—to use Johnson's phrase—"will fail somewhere." He had little sympathy for the doctrine of perfectibility—"the nature of the world will not admit of it—the inhabitants of the world will correspond to itself."[184] He criticizes Dilke as a "Godwin perfectibility man";[185] and it will be remembered that Dilke, according to Keats, "cannot feel he has a personal identity unless he has made up his Mind about everything," that he approached life with a predetermined conception of it, obtruding his own character and his own views, and that he would thus "never come at a truth as long as he lives." The only way to arrive at truth "is to make up one's mind about nothing—to let the mind be a thoroughfare for all thoughts,"[186] and to accept man individually, with all the absurdity, pathos, and nobility woven into his every speech, action, thought, and aspiration; for there is something fine in his animal instinctiveness:

> The greater part of Men make their way with the same instinctiveness, the same unwandering eye from their purposes, the same animal eagerness as the Hawk—The Hawk wants a Mate, so does the Man—look at them both they set about it and procure on[e] in the same manner—They want both a nest and they both set about one in the same manner—they get their food in the same manner—The noble animal Man for his amusement smokes his pipe—the Hawk balances about the Clouds—that is the only difference of their leisures. [...]—there is an ellectric [sic] fire in human nature tending to purify—so that among these human creature[s] there is continually some birth of a new heroism—[...] This is the very thing in which consists poetry; [...][187]

And it is as a "poor forked creature" that the philosophy of *Negative Capability* accepts man; but it detects as well, or rather it intuits, in this "same animal eagerness," in this instinctive working towards a purpose, the beauty of man, his peculiar identity, his truth.

In a letter to his brother Tom, during the Scotch tour, Keats is describing an old peasant woman:

> Squab and lean she sat and puff'd out the smoke while two ragged tattered Girls carried her along—What a thing would be the history of her Life and sensations.[188]

And few things delighted Keats more than a phrase or a passage which could reveal with a flash of intuition the history of the "life and sensations," the character, the real self, whether of an object or a person. He crossed out a remark of Johnson's quoted at the conclusion of *Antony and Cleopatra* in his copy of Shakespeare:

> The power of delighting is derived principally from the frequent changes of the scene; for, except the feminine arts, some of which are too low, which distinguish Cleopatra, no character is strongly discriminated.

This he crossed out and wrote beneath Charmian's farewell to her dead mistress, whom she is about to follow—lines which he had strongly underscored in the text, and which contain a startling imaginative revelation of character:

> Your crown's awry;
> I'll mend it, and then play.[189]

He underscored the highly self-revealing order given by Regan after the blinding of Gloucester:

> Go, thrust him out at the gates, and let him smell
> His way to Dover.[190]

And in his copy of Matheo Alemán's *The Rogue, or the Life of Guzman de Alfarache*, he underlined the words, "*His voice lowd and shrill but not very cleere*," and wrote in the margin, "This puts me in mind of

Fielding's Fanny '*whose teeth were white but uneven*'; it is the same sort of personality. The great man in this way is Chaucer."[191]

And Keats's own character was highly charged with that zest for the living which made Chaucer, when the Alchemist came riding up to join the Pilgrims, cry out with glee, "But it was joye for to seen hym swete!"[192] It was instinct with the same delight in the particular—with what Professor Lowes has called Chaucer's "eager appetence [...] for life, to which nothing was common or unclean."[193] And that which held his fascination, which fed his delight, which was indeed the very stuff of poetry—and of truth—for Keats, was the living force at work beneath every phenomenon. In the chapter on Lear in his copy of Hazlitt's *Characters of Shakespear's Plays*, he both sidemarked and underlined a passage which, he wrote in the margin, "has to a great degree the hieroglyphic visioning":

> We see the ebb and flow of the feeling, its pauses and feverish starts, its impatience of opposition, its accumulating force when it has time to recollect itself, the manner in which it avails itself of every passing word or gesture, its haste to repel insinuation, the alternate contraction & dilatation of the soul.[194]

And it was precisely this "ebb and flow of the feeling," this "alternate contraction and dilatation of the soul," this "same animal eagerness" that underlies the "alertness of a Stoat or the anxiety of a Deer," glimpsed momentarily—to return to Severn's account of his walks with Keats—in the "motions of the wind—*just how it took certain tall flowers,*" in "the smile on one child's face," in the "furtive animalism" in the faces of the passing vagrants—it was this hidden intention and movement which Keats called the "electric fire,"[195] equally at work within an Iago or an Imogen, in a sparrow or a billiard-ball, which gives every object and every creature the life which is its identity and its peculiar meaning, and which can be grasped only by an intuitive fellow-feeling on the part of the poet—this was for Keats both Beauty and Truth and, as he insisted—to turn at last to the conclusion of the "Ode on a Grecian Urn"—

> That is all
> Ye know on earth, and all ye need to know.

But this intensity for Keats was imprisoned within the concrete, and the concrete was a part of its nature and its truth. The true benefactors of humanity, said Moneta in the revised "Hyperion,"

> are no dreamers weak,
> They seek no wonder but the human face.

And Keats learned to seek no greater wonder. "Think of the Earth," said Moneta once again; and Keats, who loved the lowlands and was content to remain there, thought of the earth: he accepted it; he "served Mammon."

Endnotes

1 November 22, 1817. *Letters of John Keats*, ed. M.B. Forman (New York: 1935) 227–8. Cited hereafter as *Letters*.

2 Henri Bergson, *L'Évolution Créatrice* (Paris: 1908) 197. In English: Henri Bergson, *Creative Evolution*, tr. Arthur Mitchell (New York: 1911) 181–2.

3 Ibid., 223. In English: 204.

4 Ibid., 191–2. In English: 176.

5 Ibid., 169. In English: 155.

6 Ibid., 190–1. In English: 176.

7 Ibid., 192. In English: 177. Cf. R. A. Scott-James, *The Making of Literature* (New York: 1930) 158–9. "Art in its very nature is creative. It is synthetic, not analytic. The power which is purely analytical is dumbfounded when it seeks to account for a power which is synthetic or creative. It may indeed 'account' for it; but in so doing it looks under, and over, and round, but never *at* the secret it ought to discover; in its scientific retorts it burns up the life whose principle it sets out to isolate and reveal, and exposes no more than the charred remnants of forms that have been deprived of their vitality."

8 *Letters*, 227–8. (To Woodhouse, October 27, 1818.)

9 William Hazlitt, *Lectures on the English Poets. Collected Works* (London: 1902) V. 48.

10 See Keats's reference to his publisher, Taylor, as a "consequitive man." (*Letters*, 91. To Taylor, January 30, 1818.) Cf. also his discussion of Dilke's

character. (Ibid., 426. To George and Georgiana Keats, September 17–27, 1819.)

11 *Letters*, 72. (To George and Thomas Keats, December 21, 1817.)

12 That is, Godwin's *Political Justice*.

13 Letter not extant.

14 *Letters*, 426. (To George and Georgiana Keats, September 17–27, 1819.)

15 Ibid., 96. (To Reynolds, February 3, 1818.)

16 See Bergson, *L'Évolution Créatrice*, 195–201. In English: 179–85.

17 Cf. Hazlitt, *English Comic Writers. Collected Works*, VIII, 109. "This intuitive perception of the hidden analogies of things, or, as it may be called, this *instinct of the imagination*, is, perhaps, what stamps the character of genius on the productions of art more than any other circumstance; for it works unconsciously like nature, and receives its impressions from a kind of inspiration."

18 This sentence, as punctuated in the original, is not so clear as one could wish. I have adopted the punctuation suggested by Mr. L. J. Potts in *The Times Literary Supplement* for May 20, 1926, 339 (quoted in M.B. Forman's edition of the *Letters*, 317n). The passage, as originally punctuated, reads: "Even here though I myself am pursuing the same instinctive course as the veriest human animal you can think of—I am however young writing at random—straining at particles in the midst of a great darkness—without knowing the bearing of any one assertion of any one opinion, yet may I not in this be free from sin."

19 *Letters*, 316–7. (To George and Georgiana Keats, February 14–May 3, 1819.) Cf. "Lines to Fanny" (11–7):

> My muse had wings,

And ever ready was to take her course
Whither I bent her force,
Unintellectual, yet divine to me: —
Divine, I say! What sea-bird o'er the sea
Is a philosopher the while he goes

Winging along where the great water throes?

20 See Keats's statement, "Axioms in philosophy are not axioms until they are proved upon our pulses." *Letters*, 142. (To Reynolds, May 3, 1818.)

21 *Biographia Literaria*, ed. George Sampson (Cambridge, England: 1920) 178.

22 Cf. the first of Hazlitt's *Lectures on the English Poets*, "On Poetry in General," which Keats probably heard: Poetry "is strictly the language of the imagination; and the imagination is that faculty which represents objects, not as they are in themselves, but as they are moulded by other thoughts and feelings into an infinite variety of shapes and combinations of Power." (*Collected Works*, V. 4.) "For the end and use of poetry, both at the first and now, was and is to hold the mirror up to nature, seen through the medium of passion and imagination, not divested of that medium by means of literal truth or abstract reason." (Ibid., V, 8)

23 *Letters*, 31. (To Haydon, May 10–1, 1817.)

24 "Epistle to John Hamilton Reynolds" 74–7.

25 *Coleridge's Shakespearean Criticism*, ed. T. M. Raysor (Cambridge, MA: 1930) I, 198.

26 *Letters*, 96. (February 3, 1818.)

27 *Letters*, 426. (To George and Georgiana Keats, September 17–27, 1819.)

28 Ibid., 72. (To George and Thomas Keats, December 21, 1817.)

29 29 "Epistle to John Hamilton Reynolds" 82–5.

30 *Letters*, 67. (November 22, 1817.)

31 "On Mr. Wordsworth's *Excursion.*" *Collected Works*, I, 114.

32 *Letters*, 227. (To Woodhouse, October 27, 1818.)

33 Ibid., 107. (To George and Thomas Keats, February 21, 1818.)

34 Cf. "On Mr. Wordsworth's *Excursion*" op. cit. "He may be said to create his own materials: his thoughts are his real subject. His understanding broods over that which is without form and void; and 'makes it pregnant.' He sees all things in himself. [...] The image is lost in the sentiment." (*Collected Works*, I, 112.) Cf. also: "There is, in fact, in Mr. Wordsworth's mind an evident repugnance to admit anything that tells for itself, without the interpretation of the poet,—a fastidious antipathy to immediate effect,—a systematic unwillingness to share the palm with his subject." (Ibid., I, 114.) Keats often dined with Hazlitt, and it is highly probable, on such occasions, that Wordsworth was often the subject of their conversation.

35 Cf. Hazlitt: "His understanding *broods* over that which is without form and void."

36 *Letters*, 96–7. (February 3, 1818.)

37 Ibid., 227. (To Woodhouse, October 27, 1818.)

38 Ibid., 104. (February 19, 1818.)

39 *Letters*, 241. (To George and Georgiana Keats, October 14-31, 1818.)

40 Ibid., 69. (To Bailey, November 22, 1817.)

41 Ibid., 103-104. (To Reynolds, February 19, 1818.)

42 Ibid., 87–8. (To Bailey, January 23, 1818, and to George and Thomas Keats, January 23, 1818.)

43 Ibid., 87.

44 *Lectures on the English Poets. Collected Works*, V, –48.

45 *Letters*, 72. (To George and Thomas Keats, December 21, 1817.)

46 Ibid., 227–8. (October 27, 1818.)

47 William James, also, in discussing Shakespeare's capacity for identifying himself with his subject, has insisted upon the essentially intuitive and unconscious fashion in which the identification is accomplished. See *Principles of Psychology* (New York: 1890) II, 362–3.

48 "Ode to a Nightingale" 74.

49 *Letters*, 111. (To Bailey, March 13, 1818.)

50 Ibid., 53. (To Bailey, October 8, 1817.)

51 Ibid., 140. (To Reynolds, May 3, 1818.)

52 Ibid., 134. (To Taylor, April 24, 1818.)

53 Ibid., 137. (To Reynolds, April 27, 1818.)

54 Ibid., 142. (May 3, 1818.)

55 Ibid., 318. (February 14-May 3, 1819.)

56 Ibid., 391. (To Woodhouse, September 21, 1819.)

57 Ibid., 193. (July 18–22, 1818.)

58 *Letters*, 172.

59 "Sleep and Poetry" 101–21.

60 Ibid., 122–5.

61 *Letters*, 143–4. (To Reynolds, May 3, 1818.)

62 Ibid., 104. (To Reynolds, February 19, 1818.)

63 Ibid., 336. (To George and Georgiana Keats, February 14–May 3, 1819.)

64 See again such statements of Keats as "there is something else wanting to one who passes his life among Books" (Ibid., 137; To Reynolds, April 27, 1818) and "axioms in philosophy are not axioms until they are proved upon our pulses." (Ibid., 142, To Reynolds, May 3, 1818.)

65 See Ibid., 42, 60, 74, 134, 178, 233, 254, 258, 425; and, especially, 68, 140, 174, 223, 335, and 374.

66 It is of course well known that Keats read little formal philosophy, and it is unlikely that he was acquainted with even Hobbes, Locke, or Hume. But because of the wide vogue he enjoyed around the turn of the century, Hartley's use of the word "Sensations"—particularly in his *Observations on Man*—with its traditional Lockian meaning may well have been copied in the popular philosophical conversations of the day. Many of Keats's friends, at all events, were acquainted with Hartley. He was well known by Shelley, Wordsworth (for a discussion of the influence of Hartley on Wordsworth, see Arthur Beatty, *William Wordsworth: His Doctrine and Art in their Historical Relationships* (Madison: 1922)), and of course, Coleridge, who even named a son after him; and all three at least met Keats. Even if we discount them, however, as unlikely sources of information, there still remain Hunt and Hazlitt. Hunt was acquainted with Hartley, and Hazlitt's famous essay ("Remarks on the Systems of Hartley and Helvetius," *Collected Works*, VII, 434–75) though depreciative, is indicative of at least his interest in Hartley. Mr. Philip A. Smith has suggested to me that if Keats were indeed acquainted at all with Hartley, it was perhaps through conversation with Woodhouse; and has instanced the letter from Woodhouse to Keats of October 21, 1818 (quoted in Forman's edition of Keats's *Letters*, 225–7) in which Woodhouse mentions "our late conversation at Hesey's" in which the subject of discussion was "the ideas derivable to us from our senses singly and in their various combin[atio]ns."

67 Ibid., 336. (February 14–May 3, 1819.) Cf. Letter to Reynolds (May 3, 1818): "Here I must think that Wordsworth is deeper than Milton. [...] He *did not*

think into the human heart as Wordsworth has done." (*Letters*, 144.)

68 Ibid., 300. (February 14–May 3, 1819.)

69 Written between April 18 and November 28, 1817.

70 "Endymion" I, 1013–17.

71 Robert Bridges, "A Critical Introduction to Keats," *Collected Essays and Papers* (London: 1929) IV, 117.

72 "Hyperion" 147–9.

73 Ibid., 142.

74 *Letters*, 336. (February 14–May 3, 1819.)

75 Cf. "Endymion" I, 797–802:

> But there are
> Richer entanglements, enthrallments far
> More self-destroying, leading, by degrees,
> To the chief intensity: the crown of these
> Is made of love and friendship, and sits high
> Upon the forehead of humanity.

76 John Middleton Murry, *Keats and Shakespeare* (Oxford: 1926) 48.

77 Cf. Goethe's statement to Eckermann: "Charaktere und Ansichten lösen sich als Seiten des Dichters von ihm ab und berauben ihm für ferner Productionen der Fülle." *Eckermann's Gesprache mit Goethe* (Leipzig: 1837) 56. (September 18, 1823.) "Character and views detach themselves as sides from the poet's mind, and deprive him of the fullness requisite for future productions." *Conversations of Goethe with Johann Peter Eckermann* (Cambridge, MA: 1998) 9.

78 See John Ruskin, *Modern Painters* ("Of the Pathetic Fallacy"), *Complete Works*, eds. Cook & Wedderburn (London: 1904) V, 205–6.

79 Cf. "The poet and the dreamer are distinct, Diverse, sheer opposites, antipodes." ("Fall of Hyperion" 199–200.)

80 Ibid., 161–4.

81 Ibid., 168–9.

82 *Letters*, 140. (To Reynolds, May 3, 1818.)

83 Ibid., 53. (To Bailey, October 8, 1817.)

84 *Principles of Psychology*, II, 365–6: "But if you ask your most educated friend why he prefers Titian to Paul Veronese you will hardly get more of a reply; and you will probably get absolutely none if you inquire why Beethoven reminds him of Michael Angelo, or how it comes that a bare figure with unduly flexed joints [...] can so suggest the moral tragedy of life. His thought obeys a *nexus*, but cannot name it. And so it is with all those judgments of *experts*, which even though unmotivated are so valuable. [...] The reason lies imbedded, but not yet laid bare, in all the countless previous cases dimly suggested by the actual one, all calling up the same conclusion, which the adept thus finds himself swept on to, he knows not how or why."

85 See John Henry Newman, *An Essay in Aid of a Grammar of Assent* (London: 1891). The universe, says Newman, is essentially non-logical in nature; and those premises which the logic constructs are assumptions, not realities. Certainty may be reached, not through logic, but through the "illative sense" (343–83), which is a cumulation of past experiences, all too fine and subtle to avail separately, but which, when joined together, act intuitively and with unerring exactitude.

86 *Letters*, 69. (To Bailey, November 22, 1817.)

87 A.C. Bradley, *Oxford Lectures on Poetry* (London: 1907) 237.

88 Quoted in H. Buxton Forman, *Complete Works of John Keats* (London: 1883) III, 19.

89 See Keats's letter to Taylor, April 24, 1818 (*Letters*, 134): "I find there is no worthy pursuit but the idea of doing some good to the world—" See also "Fall of Hyperion" 199 and 201-202:

> "The poet and the dreamer are distinct,
> . . . .
> The one pours out a balm upon the world,
> The other vexes it."

90 "Sleep and Poetry" 124–5.

91 See Keats's Letter to Shelley (*Letters*, 507, August, 1820): "A modern work it is said must have a purpose, which may be the God—*an artist* must serve Mammon—"

92 *Letters*, 71. (To George and Thomas Keats, December 21, 1817.)

93 Ibid., 507. (To Shelley, August, 1820.)

94 Three similarly concrete revisions may be instanced from the manuscript of the ode "To Autumn": "Who hath not seen thee? for thy haunts are many" was changed to "Who hath not seen thee *oft amid thy stores*?" "Or sound asleep in a half reaped *field*" became "Or on a *half-reap'd furrow* sound asleep"; and "Spares for one slumberous minute the next swath" was transformed to "Spares the next swath *and all its twinèd flowers*."

95 "It *aches* in loneliness" ("Isabella" xxviii, 4).

> "It made sad Isabella's eyelids *ache*" (Ibid., xlvi, 7).
> "To think how they may *ache* in icy hoods
> and mails" ("Eve of St. Agnes" ii, 9).
> "Or I shall drowse beside thee, so my soul
> doth *ache*" (Ibid., xxxi, 9).
> "One hand she pressed upon that *aching*
> spot" ("Hyperion" I, 42).
> "O *aching* time! O moments big as years!
> ("Hyperion" I, 64).

"But horrors, portion'd to a giant nerve,
Oft made Hyperion *ache*" (Ibid., I, 175–6).
"So saw he *panting* light" ("Endymion" II, 883).
"a *panting* glow" (Ibid., II, 970).
"our souls in one eternal *pant*" ("O that a week could be an age" 1.12).
"and stars drew in their *panting* fires" ("Lamia" I, 300).
"And make its silvery splendor *pant* with bliss" ("Hyperion" III, 102).
"For ever warm and still to be enjoy'd,
For ever *panting*, and for ever young;" ("Ode on a Grecian Urn" iii, 6–7).

A further instance of Keats's instinctive reaching for intensity, although not of quite as physical a nature, is his frequent use of the word "full," particularly in compound epithets. A few examples are:

"Bees gorge *full* their cells" ("Endymion" III, 40).
"*full*-brimm'd goblet" (Ibid., IV, 416).
"*full*-flowering weed" ("Lamia" I, 44).
"*full*-grown lambs" ("To Autumn" iii, 8).
"*full*-throated ease" ("Ode to a Nightingale" i, 10).

96 See Caroline Spurgeon, *Keats's Shakespeare* (Oxford: 1928) 17.

97 I, 2, 8–9.

98 I, 2, 176.

99 V, 1, 246–7.

100 IV, 1, 162–3.

101 Arthur Symons, *The Romantic Movement in English Poetry* (London: 1909) 307.

102 "Sleep and Poetry" 79–80.

103 "Hyperion" I, 219.

104 Ibid., I, 210.

105 "Isabella" x, 4.

106 "Ode to Psyche" 13.

107 "Hyperion" I, 206.

108 Ibid., II, 356.

109 "Ode to a Nightingale" v, 3.

110 "Fall of Hyperion" I, 6.

111 "Endymion" II, 999.

112 "Eve of St. Agnes" xvi, 3.

113 "Lamia" I, 154.

114 Keats's tendency to strengthen his images by making them tactile is well exemplified in his use, in almost every conceivable way, of the adjective "soft":

> "soft ravishment" ("Endymion" II, 715).
> "And catch soft floatings from a faint-heard hymning" ("Sleep and Poetry" 34).
> "Where we may soft humanity put on" ("Epistle to Matthew" 55).
> "With 'haviour soft" ("Endymion" IV, 464).
> "soft ascent" ("Isabella" xvi, 4).
> "soft adorings" ("Eve of St. Agnes" vi, 3).
> "soft incense" ("Ode to a Nightingale" v, 2).
> "And there shall be for thee all soft delight" ("Ode to Psyche" 64).
> "soft shades" ("Calidore" 46).
> "fragrance soft" ("Hyperion" I, 210).
> "soft crimsons" ("Cap and Bells" lxii, 5).

115 "Lines to Fanny" 4.

116 "Ode to a Nightingale" v, 1–2.

117 "Fall of Hyperion" I, 23–4

118 Ibid., I, 404.

119 Ibid., I, 98–9.

120 "Eve of St. Agnes" xiii, 5.

121 "Hyperion" I, 209–10.

122 "Ode to Psyche" 13.

123 "Eve of St. Agnes" xxxi, 4–5.

124 Robert Bridges, *Collected Essays and Papers*, IV, 169.

125 "Endymion," II, 348–50.

126 "Isabella," liii, 1–2, 5.

127 "Eve of St. Agnes," iii, 2–3.

128 Ibid., xvi, 1.

129 Ibid., xxvi, 3.

130 "Hyperion," I, 18–9.

131 Ibid., I, 74.

132 Ibid., I, 189.

133 Ibid., I, 353.

134 Ibid., III, 50.

135 "King Stephen" I, 2, 1–2.

136 "Ode to a Nightingale" vii, 7.

137 William Sharp, *Life and Letters of Joseph Severn* (London: 1892) 20.

138 *Letters*, 317. (To George Keats, February 14–May 3, 1819.)

139 *Faerie Queene*, II, xii, 23, 6. Cf. Keats's own phrase, "the *gulphing* whale" ("Endymion" III, 205).

140 Charles and Mary Cowden Clarke, *Recollections of Writers* (London: 1878) 126.

141 "Hyperion" I, 28–30.

142 "Miltonic verse can not be written but in an artful or rather artist's humour. [...] It may be interesting to you to pick out some lines from "Hyperion" and put a mark X to the false beauty proceeding from art, and one || to the true voice of feeling." *Letters*, 384–5. (To Reynolds, September 21, 1819.)

143 David Watson Rannie, *Keats's Epithets. Essays and Studies By Members of the English Association*, III (Oxford: 1912) 110–1.

144 "Hyperion" I, 74.

145 "Eve of St. Agnes" xxxvii, 3.

146 "Ode on Melancholy" ii, 7.

147 "Isabella" xxvii, 1–2.

148 Charles Lamb, "Lamia, Isabella, the Eve of St. Agnes, and Other Poems by John Keats." *Essays* (London: 1929) II, 302. See also Leigh Hunt, *Autobiography* (New York: 1850) II, 40: "I remember Lamb's delight and admiration in reading this book; how pleased he was with [...] the fine daring anticipation in that passage [...]. 'So the two brothers and their *murdered* man [...].'"

149 "Eve of St. Agnes" xxvi, 3.

150 Ibid., xxxiii, 9.

151 "Ode to Psyche" 13.

152 "Hyperion" I, 219.

153 Ibid., I, 263.

154 Ibid., II, 172.

155 "Eve of St. Agnes" xlii, 7.

156 "Isabella" xiv, 5.

157 "Ode to Psyche" 54–5.

158 John Ruskin, *Complete Works*, VII, 107–8. Or: *Modern Painters*, Vol. 5 (London: 1860) 85, footnote 1.

159 "Ode to a Nightingale" vii, 5–7.

160 "Hyperion" I, 85–6.

161 Ibid., I, 10.

162 Ibid., I, 89–90.

163 "Sleep and Poetry" 236–7.

164 *Antony and Cleopatra*, I, iii, 35.

165 Spurgeon, *Keats's Shakespeare*, 25.

166 *Letters*, 72. (To George and Thomas Keats, December 21, 1817.)

167 Ibid., 227. (To Woodhouse, October 27, 1818.)

168 A. C. Bradley, *Oxford Lectures on Poetry*, 211.

169 *Letters*, 111. (To Bailey, March 13, 1818.)

170 Ibid., 439–0. (To Taylor, November 17, 1819.)

171 Quoted in H. B. Forman's edition of Keats's *Letters*, Preface, xv. Cf. Landor's letter to Lord Houghton: "Of all our poets excepting Shakespeare and Milton, and perhaps Chaucer, he [Keats] has the most of the poetical character—fire, fancy, and diversity. [...] There is an effluence of power and light pervading all his works, and a freshness such as we feel in the glorious dawn of Chaucer." Quoted in Sir Sidney Colvin, *John Keats* (London: 1918) 537. Cf. also *Landor, English Visiter, and Florentine Visiter*: "Since the time of Chaucer there have been only two poets who at all resemble him; and these two are widely dissimilar one from the other, Burns and Keats." *Imaginary Conversations*, ed. C.G. Crump (London: 1891) VI, 45n. Or: *The Works of Walter Savage Landor*, Vol. 1 (London: 1846) 337.

172 *Letters*, 454. (To Georgiana Augusta Keats, January 17, 1820.)

173 Ibid., 455.

174 A.C. Bradley, *Oxford Lectures on Poetry*, 220.

175 *Letters*, 228. (To Woodhouse, October 27, 1818.)

176 Ibid., 216. (To Dilke, September 21, 1818.)

177 *Love's Labour's Lost*, IV, iii, 338.

178 *Letters*, 65. (To Reynolds, November 22, 1817.)

179 Woodhouse's *Scrapbook*. Quoted in C.L. Finney, *Evolution of Keats's Poetry* (Cambridge, MA: 1936) II, 492.

180 *Letters*, 129. (To Haydon, April 8, 1818.)

181 *Troilus and Criseyde*, V, 1172. *Chaucer's Complete Works*, ed. F. N. Robinson (Cambridge, MA: 1933) 555.

182 *Letters*, 401. (To George Keats, September 17–27, 1819.)

183 "Man is originally a 'poor forked creature' subject to the same mischances as the beasts of the forest, destined to hardships and disquietude of some kind or other." (*Letters*, 335. To George and Georgiana Keats, February 14–May 3, 1819.) See *King Lear*, III, iv, 110, 111.

184 Ibid., 335.

185 Ibid., 426. (To George and Georgiana Keats, September 17–27, 1819.)

186 Loc. cit.

187 Ibid., 316. (To George Keats, February 14–May 3, 1819.)

188 Ibid., 174. (To Thomas Keats, July 3–9, 1818.)

189 Spurgeon, *Keats's Shakespeare*, 32. (*Antony and Cleopatra*, V, ii, 320–1.)

190 Ibid., 50. (*King Lear*, III, vii, 93-94.)

191 Amy Lowell, *John Keats* (New York: 1925) Appendix C, II, 583.

192 *Canon's Yeoman's Prologue*, 579. *Chaucer's Complete Works*, ed. F.N. Robinson, 255.

193 John Livingston Lowes, *Geoffrey Chaucer and the Development of his Genius* (New York: 1934) 238.

194 William Hazlitt, *Characters of Shakespear's Plays* (London: 1817) 157. This is now in the Lowell Collection in the Harvard College Library.

195 *Letters*, 316. (To George Keats, February 14–May 3, 1819.)

GPSR Authorized Representative: Easy Access System Europe, Mustamäe tee 50, 10621 Tallinn, Estonia, gpsr.requests@easproject.com

www.ingramcontent.com/pod-product-compliance
Ingram Content Group UK Ltd.
Pitfield, Milton Keynes, MK11 3LW, UK
UKHW012153200826
474551UK00004B/45
* 9 7 8 1 9 7 1 5 5 9 3 8 4 *